PRAISE FOR REGINA CATES
AND *LEAD WITH YOUR HEART*

"If I were asked to share one life lesson, it would be to lead with your heart—exactly as Regina Cates teaches us in her beautiful book. Cates gives us the keys to creating a joyful life: Find your connection with heart and reclaim the wonder of who you really are. What a magnificent mix of inspiration, wisdom, and humility this book is!"
—Tavis Smiley, PBS broadcaster, author, and philanthropist

"This book is like a note from a close friend, reporting on her spiritual journey from lovelessness to love. By walking you through her experiences, she casts light on your own. And not just her life, but yours too begins to change."
—Marianne Williamson, #1 *New York Times* bestselling author of *A Return to Love*

"Regina Cates has done a huge service by lighting the path for us to reconnect with our heart. Cates has made the journey herself, and each chapter resounds with her painful, all-too-human experience. Easy to read, yet filled with wisdom that will penetrate your heart, this book puts the power back in your hands. It's a must-have."
—Marci Shimoff, #1 *New York Times* bestselling author of *Happy for No Reason* and *Love for No Reason*

"Regina Cates is a beautiful human being who teaches us by sharing her own life-changing experiences. Her message is loud and clear: Trust your heart; it will never lead you astray."
—don Miguel Ruiz, MD, #1 *New York Times* bestselling author of *The Four Agreements*

"In *Lead with Your Heart*, Cates provides factual evidence that the heart is a wise spiritual organ that beats in rhythm to being true to oneself in a most noble way: living a heart-centered life."
—Michael Bernard Beckwith, founder of Agape Spiritual Center and author of *Life Visioning*

"*Lead with Your Heart* is an important contribution to the expansion of consciousness and the evolution of life. This clearly written book enables us to look at our lives from a different perspective, and in doing so, to sense the dazzling resplendence of life. Regina's words teach us to lead with our heart. The clarity that comes from the heart guides us to greater love, service, and wisdom. Every page of this book will open you to your heart: your best self, your highest potential, and your greatest joy."

—Jorge Luis Delgado, Peruvian shaman and author of
Andean Awakening: An Inca Guide to Mystical Peru

"At a time when we most need it, Regina Cates has created a tour de force with *Lead with Your Heart*. In this down-to-earth guide, Cates speaks to us like a wise friend, showing us how to align the physical with the spiritual to promote optimum health, joy in our relationships, and peace in our heart. It just may be the best book I've read this year."

—Uzzi Reiss, MD, OB/GYN, founder of the Beverly Hills Anti-Aging
Center, and author of *The Natural Superwoman*

"Regina's transformative book is a powerful awareness-raising tool I am eager to share with therapy, counseling, and coaching clients as well as my own family and friends. We are challenged to courageously evaluate and purposefully reflect on our life choices, while also encouraged and reassured that making the effort to do so will be an empowering experience that is well worth it. A buffet of wisdom nuggets, free of confusing jargon and replete with genuine, relatable examples from the author's life, there is something for everyone here. This is a must-read for anyone serious about maximizing their potential, peace, balance, and life satisfaction!"

—Gail D. Simon-Boyd, PhD, licensed psychologist,
adjunct psychology instructor, and wellness coach

"Regina Cates has given us a tremendous gift by sharing her heart on these pages. This book is for everyone who is attempting to make meaning of his or her life, for everyone who is looking for a guide on how to live the best life given the circumstances, for everyone who is desiring self-acceptance, joy, and peace while fully experiencing this crazy world we live in. I can personally attest to how leading with my heart is helping me become a more centered, joyful, truthful, and fully alive person, accepting—and even embracing—my personal journey. It doesn't matter if you don't 'do' the new age stuff, have a million self-help books, or think spirituality isn't your forte. Get this book anyway."

—Sharmila Devar, actress

LEAD WITH
YOUR HEART

Hier⊕phantpublishing

REGINA CATES

Cover design by Adrian Morgan
Cover art by © Valeriy Lebedev | Shutterstock
Interior design by Jane Hagaman

Hierophant Publishing
8301 Broadway, Suite 219
San Antonio, TX 78209
888-800-4240
www.hierophantpublishing.com

If you are unable to order this book from your local bookseller, you may order directly from the publisher.

Library of Congress Control Number: 2013956298

ISBN: 978-1-938289-28-6

10 9 8 7 6 5 4 3 2 1
Printed on acid-free paper in the United States of America

The figure on page 14 of twenty-five black blocks is from Scientific Psychic: www.scientificpsychic.com/graphics.

The pyramid and heart figures on pages 90 and 176 are by Miguel Bravo.

To Barbara Rose Simon,
for her faith, patience, and unwavering support.

For many years I was terrified of dying.

Then one day I realized I was really afraid of living.

Contents

Introduction

My name is Regina, and I am creating an incredible life filled with love, compassion, and purpose. But I was not always the joyful, confident, and responsible person I am today.

On my forty-third birthday, I remember sitting on the couch with my dogs huddled around me, rapidly going through a box of tissues and about to open a second. The tears did not stop. I sobbed because it was my birthday and life sucked. I felt helpless and hopeless; I wanted someone to heal me, someone to complete me. Without someone to rescue me and cheer me on, I did not imagine much chance for contentment.

Longing to have a good, lifelong relationship with a partner, I grew up believing I would meet the person of my dreams, enjoy a deep, rewarding, lasting relationship, and somehow magically live happily ever after. After a particularly difficult breakup—my sixth in a series of not-good relationships—it became crystal clear I did not know how to be a strong half of a healthy relationship. The bottom line was this: I did not love myself, so I did not know how to love others.

It seemed my life was a failure.

For so many years, I went along with the idea of success as defined by my peers and society, which meant having attained wealth, position, and honors. In order to be a success, I got a good education. Then I landed a series of respectable jobs with great benefits and, at some of them, a big corner office. Although I did not dislike my jobs, I was not content. My days were jam-packed with work, leaving little time for anything else. My overcrowded schedule cost me relationships with my partner, friends, pets, and myself. I had no time to really enjoy life. I was too busy being a success.

Where I lived, what I drove, what I wore, what I owned, and what I did determined my worth. I had a great house with a big mortgage, stylish furniture, and a well-landscaped yard, and yet I was unable to afford to have my dog's teeth cleaned. My car was beautiful, but I could not pay for its regular maintenance. The fancy wardrobe I thought was necessary for my successful image caused me to not keep up with, much less pay off, mounting debt.

With all of my success came large debt from living beyond my means. My home was crammed with stuff, and yet my heart was empty. Filled with fear and worry, I could not imagine how I was going to pay off all the bills, even with my good job. After almost drowning in debt, I realized that "keeping up with the Joneses" was a shallow and irresponsible endeavor.

From an early age, I felt as if I were molded into a purchasing machine. Product ads promised to make me contented, beautiful, or sexy, and I spent much of my life surrounding myself with things, since I was conditioned to believe my house, my car, and my job defined me. I thought things would make me happy. So, I got used to whipping out the credit card without caring about how I was going to pay when the bill arrived. Nor did I stop to question if chasing after things was actually the way to joy or peace of mind.

During a visit to the veterinarian, I learned one of my dogs had a heart problem because of poor dental health. The news hit me like a ton of bricks. How could I love my pets and not take care of their health needs? Without proper care, they would not have the quality of life I wanted for them. Saying I loved them without responsibly demonstrating care for their health showed me my priorities were not straight.

What was the purpose of having a luxury car if I could not afford to keep it in proper working order? When had my car changed from being a mode of transportation to a status symbol? How important was my wardrobe, furniture, or manicured lawn if each time I got dressed, sat on my sofa, or spent time outdoors I felt stress in the pit of my stomach? Who was I trying to impress? Even if others were impressed by my materialistic focus, I was frustrated, anxious, and exhausted by such a superficial and unrealistic standard.

When I took time to honestly think about why I was spending without awareness or concern, it allowed me to step out of ego-motivated consumerism. As long as I continued to live above my means, I was going to be stuck with that horrible feeling. Buying more stuff would not validate me or get people to like me for who I really was.

Then I lost my job, and it all came crashing down. My excellent education and successful employment record did not help me find another position quickly, and it was almost two years before I was employed again.

I had not foreseen this and was totally unprepared. I sold my home to live off the equity and moved in with my parents. I let go of the beautiful garden I loved. My success seemed to quickly turn to failure.

And there was my health. . . . I'd stopped making regular exercise a priority around my twenty-fifth birthday, and for more than twenty-two years I'd smoked cigarettes. As a rock 'n' roll drummer, the advice I'd received to protect my hearing went in one ear and out the other. I burned the candle at both ends and went for days with only a few hours of sleep each night.

As a weekend landscape designer, I loaded, hauled, and installed objects much too heavy for my strength and size. On my days off, I sunbathed without protection, often resulting in some bad burns. Fast-food restaurants were my personal chef for far too long. Water did not place on my list of top ten beverages. And sugar was a Federal Drug Administration vital food group. As you might imagine from all this, getting regular health and dental checkups was not a top priority. The only thing I was consistently protective of was my eyesight, because without regular eye exams and glasses I would not have been allowed to drive legally.

Then, at about forty-two, my life plan did a one-eighty. Not once had it occurred to me that there might come a day when I would become physically impaired. Sure, I thought about getting lung cancer, to the point where I was obsessed and lived in terror of it. I got sick all the time, smelled bad, and had a constant cough. But it hadn't occurred to me that any greater physical challenge might lie ahead. Why would it? I was born a natural athlete, excelling at every sport I attempted. Working in the yard, moving heavy loads of soil, plants, and stone, was a challenging pleasure. Eventually all the years of lifting too many heavy objects without supporting my lower back or asking for help caught up with me.

Unaware that my back was unstable and teetering on the brink of disaster, I sneezed. That one sneeze resulted in a lower back disc herniation, and the pain went from uncomfortable to excruciating over the next few days. Fortunately, I worked for a neurosurgeon at the time, so I got a quick referral and was rushed into surgery.

Two weeks after the surgery, I was able to walk around a short block in my neighborhood. It took four weeks for me to drive and six weeks to return to work. More than three years later, I finally woke up and accepted the truth: my body was not going to ever be the same.

The most substantial shock I received in life was looking in the mirror and not recognizing the person looking back. Two back-to-back surgeries on my spine left me with permanent nerve damage, muscle atrophy, and a limp. It became easy to ignore the inner, aware voice that told me to keep exercising, eat right, and stretch. Instead, I ate without awareness, sat around feeling sorry for myself, and waited for a miracle.

I gained more than fifty pounds in what seemed like the blink of an eye, but it was actually not overnight. As I became emotionally detached from being responsible for my body, time got lost within my unconscious excuses.

At forty-three years old, on that couch, rehashing all that was wrong with my life, I felt destined to be miserable and lonely. I was fully caught up in the largest pity party I had ever hosted when something extraordinary happened. Originating from deep within my soul, the words *Do you enjoy feeling this way?* passed through my consciousness. "Of course not!" I screamed out loud to no one. My heart responded, *Who do you think is actually responsible for creating the joyful and fulfilling life you want?*

In the instant it took for "I am" to roll off my lips, the idea that someone outside me had the power to fix my life or heal the holes within my heart vanished. I became empowered by the truth. Creating the life I wanted was completely an inside job. If I am my own worst enemy, how can I be my own best friend? I was the only one capable of developing the self-love, intimacy, self-acceptance, peace, and joy for which I longed.

I could no longer blame other people for my life. Yes, growing up had been hard. At school and in church I was bullied and oppressed, causing me to be angry, blaming, and unhappy.

Feelings of unworthiness, confusion, and rejection resulted in an unhealthy and deeply wounded sense of self (ego). My suffering and immature side was not interested in being accountable for *my* actions or emotions.

That day I began accepting the reality that my life remained difficult and unsatisfying because I still saw myself, other people, and the world around me through the eyes of a damaged and emotionally immature child. Allowing hurt to speak for me, to behave for me, to think for me, I was being driven by inappropriate impulses.

A thoughtless and reactive approach did not allow me to create a happy, peaceful, and rewarding life. Only ugliness came from self-centeredness.

Through self-assessment, I realized that living insensitively is being out of control. If I am not emotionally in charge of and present with my behavior, I undesirably and recklessly react rather than take the thoughtful actions necessary to create the productive life I say I want.

It took time, heartache, frustration, and disappointment to learn that when I practiced reactionary and self-justifying behavior, I usually received the same in return. Unfavorable action carries baggage in the form of damaging consequences. The returning result may not happen right away, yet the energy expended is guaranteed to be returned.

There is truth to the saying "Payback is hell." The difference between constructive and destructive behavior is freedom from the suffering of reprisal that results from irresponsible actions.

What a revelation! What a wonderful birthday gift!

Now on September 4th each year, I celebrate the day I was born. When the gathering is over and friends and family leave, I retreat to a quiet place. Spending a few moments alone, I pay tribute to my forty-third birthday, the day I began ending my suffering by looking within to find the biggest fan, most loving life partner, and best friend I will ever have. That is the "birth-day" I began to live—the day I chose my heart's path.

Learning to lead with my heart—that often hard-to-describe yet fully understood part of me where the positive guiding principles of a conscious life, such as responsibility, cooperation, and peacefulness originate—has transformed my life. No, it hasn't always been easy or smooth. I've made lots of mistakes. But along the way I've learned to love myself and found a loving partner. I learned to respect myself and stopped smoking and lost those extra fifty pounds. I learned to put self-centeredness, blame, judgment, and feeling like a victim behind me. I learned to create a life of deep meaning by leading with the respectful, compassionate, and sensitive part of me.

Assuming responsibility for my life has filled me with self-love, joy, and satisfaction. Now, instead of crying on the couch with my dogs, I celebrate life. And I want you to celebrate life by learning to lead with your heart, too.

In the following pages I'll share stories, some funny and embarrassing, some sad and poignant, but all of them hopefully inspiring. These are the lessons I learned, the questions I asked, the mistakes I made, the limitations I overcame, and the realizations I had that moved me from living egoistically and irresponsibly to putting my accountable heart out front.

Following your heart's path is an adventure of creating a life of deep meaning. My greatest desire is that this will serve as an indispensable guidebook to help you along the way. That is why at the end of each chapter, I offer some meditations and exercises to help spark your personal reflections.

If you have a journal, write down your answers there. If you don't own a journal, jot down your responses here in the spaces and margins. However you prefer, thinking about these questions for yourself and applying them to your own life as I applied them to mine will go a long way in helping you lead with your heart.

While I do not know your personality, beliefs, likes, and dislikes, I do know you and I are more alike than different. Please consider this book the testimonial of a good friend. Regardless of what pain and disappointment you have experienced, you can have self-acceptance and self-worth. You can love yourself and be loved by others. You can live in peace with your family, neighbors, co-workers, and the folks you meet each day.

So if you're ready, let's begin the journey.

Question the Path You Are On

Self-love, respect, and inner peace come from learning how to travel through life in the easiest and most fulfilling manner. Finding the path of least resistance requires accepting it is your actions that create your life. Through self-assessment, you identify those aspects of your behavior, beliefs, judgments, and fears that are preventing you from creating the life you truly want.

Confronting your behavior is not nearly as difficult a process as you may believe. Yes, it takes time to be comfortable looking candidly at yourself. At first, what you consider faults stand out under the bright lights of self-evaluation. So you may tell yourself it is easier not to look. Yet, if you do not look at yourself, it is impossible to see what you *do* like about you. Without self-assessment it is also impossible to identify those aspects of yourself that you do not like but can change.

Getting to the heart of the matter of self-change requires shifting your ego's focus from the laundry list of what everyone else needs to do to make your life easier to concentrating on what you can change about youself. To begin moving past your ego's resistance to change, ask yourself these questions:

- Do you own your behavior, or do you pass the buck for your actions? *No, Yes I do with myself*
- Do you evaluate yourself and others based on seeking *ego's* facts, or do you allow reactive ego to jump to judgment? *Judgment*
- Are you blindly following the beliefs of others, or do you seek to establish your own? *following others*
- Does fear keep you tied up in knots, or have you chosen to walk in faith? *Yes, fear keeps me tied up in knots*

Don't be upset or judgmental if what you discover is disappointing. There was a time I was not the person I told myself I was. Today I am the person I always wanted to be only because I took time to determine what was *not* right about me.

Only when you know what needs changing can you change your path, so your life changes for the better. Positive change begins by being truthful with you, about you. Intentionally looking within, you reach the understanding of who you are, what you value, what about yourself is going right, what is not going right, and what wounds need to heal.

Questioning the path you are on allows you to become aware of and eventually break free from unconscious behavior patterns. By honestly looking at yourself, your heart begins to take the lead in creating your life.

I need to love myself, d be confiednt in who I am. I need to open up more, I need to own my behavior, Dont feed on negativoldy

Own Your Behavior

While out and about in the neighborhood with my dog Madison, a corgi-shelty rescue, I noticed a group of young men walking toward me. They were talking loudly and pushing each other around. Shoulder to shoulder, they moved in a tight, five-abreast formation that spanned the entire width of the sidewalk, leaving no room for anyone who may have been approaching from the opposite direction.

With a cup of hot coffee in one hand and Madison's leash in the other, I continued walking. As we steadily moved toward each other, I realized there was nothing for me to do except stop. The group, seemingly unaware of my presence, did not break rank. At the last possible second, a young man bumped into me, and my dog and I were forced off the sidewalk and into the street. The group did not stop. The young men did not look back as they went on their way. I silently collected myself, my dog, and what was left of my coffee.

In the past, chances are good I would have impulsively reacted to the young men, pointing out their inconsiderate behavior with something profound, such as, "Hey, assholes! Didn't you see me? You are rude, selfish little jerks." This time I did not. Today, I own my behavior.

Several years before "road rage" became a popular description for those who express themselves in this manner, I had an especially memorable encounter. I noticed a car speeding up behind me on the interstate. I was in the center lane, and the lanes on either side of me were empty.

In no time the car was upon me. The driver began honking. After a few seconds he moved his car into the left lane, came alongside me, and gestured with a rude hand signal. Then he sped up, got in front of me, and slowed down. Irritated by his rude behavior, I honked and returned the hand signal. Then he moved back into the left lane, came alongside me, and flipped me the bird again, with more anger. I got scared. Fear for my safety caused me to seek a quick end to the exchange.

Moving into the right lane, I took the first exit. He followed. I pulled into a parking lot, found an open space in front of a small store, and rushed inside. He got out of his car and trailed me. I moved rapidly to the back and hid behind some tall shelves.

The store was filled with female customers. He stood out, and after a minute he left. Both relieved and furious, I wanted the police to haul him off, lock him up, and throw away the key. As I drove away, I was completely focused on the man's actions— I didn't once question my irresponsible behavior.

For weeks I stayed angry at the man on the highway and justified stooping to his level of aggressive rudeness, even as experience proved time and again that doing so did not make me feel validated, happier, or proud. Intellectually, I knew reacting impulsively to people or the maddening situations I encountered did nothing to help me feel better or to change them. Actually, being angry made me feel worse.

I was waiting for others to transform into more responsible and courteous people before I stepped up. Still blaming and creating excuses, I had not yet accepted self-assessment as the way to identify behaviors I needed to change. Until one day, when a new door of personal accountability and self-discipline opened within my heart. This time I walked through.

It was a Friday afternoon. I was working as a college administrator and had just overheard a department secretary address a professor as *Mr.* X instead of *Dr.* X. The professor arrogantly reprimanded the secretary in front of me, and I fired back a snide comment in her defense. Immediately embarrassed about what I had just blurted out, I rationalized my behavior and hurried off to my office.

When I returned home Sunday evening from a weekend getaway, I found a lengthy e-mail from Dr. X chastising me. Of course, my initial reaction was anger. My wounded pride justified my actions. Starting down the well-worn path of the victim, I began a scathing reply, all the while thinking, *He started all this by being such an arrogant, self-absorbed ass. He may have a PhD, but he lacks the basics of civility. How in the world can he blame me for his rude, condescending behavior?*

Suddenly, something deep within me shifted. I was not able to continue. In my honest heart of hearts, I knew the time had come to address some hard truths about my behavior:

- Had I treated Dr. X as I would want to be treated? No.
- Had my rudeness accomplished anything positive? No.
- Would I feel better now if I had chosen not to engage in the first place? Yes.
- Did Dr. X's behavior change my responsibility for my own behavior? No.
- Doesn't attempting to control others really mean I am not in control of myself? Yes.

I stopped typing and deliberately asked myself these questions. That, combined with genuinely wanting to get the answers, was the jump-start my heart needed to at last overrule my defensive and offended pride. Through candid self-evaluation, I admitted my anger was, once again, not about another's behavior. Choosing to take my disappointment out on someone else was not assuming liability for my actions.

In spite of the familiar ways I tried to project my resentment and frustration onto Dr. X, the magnificent aha moment was realizing it was my guilt pointing the finger of blame in his direction. I discovered my guilt was rooted in shame for once again putting my angry, insecure, and immature side forward. I was really mad at me for not controlling myself.

To lead with my heart, I must take accountability for my actions. Turning the eye of evaluation in my own direction, I realized that being an ass is a choice, not a condition. So creating my behavior with positive purpose had each time been my choice, too. I realized that everything I do is a choice.

Another weight lifted off me the moment I accepted it is not possible to control or change anyone else's behavior. I may choose to react aggressively to the man on the interstate, or reprimand the professor for being arrogant. However, changing their behavior is entirely their job.

Yes, there are occasions when it is appropriate to respond, to take a position against the unconscious behavior of other people, or to stand up for what is right. One day I witnessed a pedestrian scream at a driver after almost being hit because the man in the car had been talking on his cell phone. The pedestrian was upset because the driver was oblivious to the danger he posed to others, as well as to himself. Yet, I learned there is a difference between protecting myself or other people from physical harm and defending my ego against the rude actions of others. Regardless of how critical, self-centered, annoying, and offensive others choose to be, I do not gain anything by engaging in ego-boxing with them to prove myself right. Keeping the bad behavior train going doesn't make me joyful or more peaceful.

Until I understood these lessons on an emotional heart level, I did not realize I was making life unnecessarily hard. I was battling like a salmon swimming upstream. The bears, rocks, and treacherous currents I encountered were the result of looking for accountability, civility, and change outside of me. The moment I chose to play nicely with the fish and other things that shared my river—regardless of how they chose to play with me—I found the self-control I'd been longing for.

Assuming responsibility for my behavior in the encounter with Dr. X changed my anger, embarrassment, and a lifetime of feeling like a victim into truly being empowered. Permanently giving up membership in the Victim of Circumstances Beyond My Control Club freed me to be the person I wanted others to see. The changes I longed for from other people were actually the changes I needed to make in me.

Another wonderful realization was that life is now. It is not possible to go back in time and undo the past. Rather than repeat the familiar pattern of regretting how poorly I behaved in my encounter with Dr. X, I chose to start fresh in the moment. This was a new day.

With my reply email to Dr. X still open, I hit the backspace key until all blame and accusation were erased and began again.

Dear Dr. X,

You are right. Please accept my sincerest apology for behaving badly. I truly regret any harm I caused you.

Sincerely,

Regina V. Cates

When I left the college, the single parting gift I received was from Dr. X. Our interaction changed me, and he will remain close to my heart. I am deeply grateful to him for being part of a great life lesson. The box of chocolates was his way of saying it had been important for him, too.

You and I cannot control or change anyone else but ourselves. How other people choose to behave is a reflection on them. People may be rude, insulting, condescending, or deceitful, and yet their behavior is a reflection of who they are. How we behave in response is a reflection of who we are. The important thing to remember is that our behavior demonstrates, to us and to others, our level of self-discipline, which reveals how much we love and respect ourselves (or not).

Positive change requires challenging ourselves. The next time you encounter a rude driver or an arrogant co-worker and you behave in a way that leaves you disappointed in yourself, be completely honest and assume accountability for your part of the exchange. Being able to admit we are wrong is the action that gets us on the right track. Holding ourselves accountable empowers us to make different, more positive choices next time.

MEDITATIONS AND EXERCISES

Sit down in a quiet place and write down your answers to these questions:

1. Do you treat other people and all living things as you want to be treated?   NO

2. On the occasions when you have reactively ego-boxed with someone, did your rudeness accomplish anything positive?   NO

3. Looking back, would you honestly feel better about yourself if you had chosen not to engage in the first place?   Yes, be more positive

Ask Yourself Hard Questions

Around the age of six, I began experiencing growing pains. Frequently I'd wake up in the middle of the night feeling very uncomfortable. My legs hurt. My arms hurt. It seemed like everything hurt. After a while, the pain would go away and I'd fall back asleep, but this lasted for a few years.

You go through a similar process as you grow out of seeing yourself as simply a human being who is run by a self-centered mind. It is through the growing pains of self-assessment that you learn about yourself, what you value, what wounds need healing, and what beliefs and behaviors are currently creating your life. Honestly looking into your heart is not easy. But it is self-loving, because standing alone in front of the mirror of candid evaluation is how you gain a clear understanding of and respect for who you are now, so you can become the person you want to be.

Often it is a painful process, especially when the identity you've created or the identity that was created for you by others clings for dear life in fear of change. After a while, with your persistent and truthful self-assessment, the pain of struggling with the attachment you have to who you believe yourself to be (ego) falls away. Your internal vision improves, and you see yourself through an expanded, clearer, more accurate heart-awareness.

At one time I thought being sarcastic was a sign I was witty, intelligent, or humorous. One day my cynicism hurt someone deeply, and she challenged me as to why I thought it was okay to be caustic. I was embarrassed and reactively defended what I thought being sarcastic meant. I was wrong.

I learned sarcasm is defined as "mocking, contemptuous, or ironic language intended to convey scorn or insult." Going back to the origins of the word, I discovered sarcasm means to "tear flesh." Being sarcastic did not mean I was clever or humorous but actually meant I was condescending, negative, and disrespectful. And that meant when my words hurt someone I was also hurting myself by irresponsibly showing my lack of self-love, self-respect, and self-control. Realizing what it really means to be sarcastic was a big wake-up call for me, one that has made all of my relationships better, more loving, and more respectful.

There also was a time when I was dishonest with myself and with other people, and this manifested in all facets of my life. When I overate, I promised myself that starting tomorrow I would begin eating less and exercising more. Tomorrow came with another excuse, and the day after that, another excuse. Even when fifty-three extra pounds resulted in a stranger looking back at me in the mirror I still was dishonest about how I'd gotten there.

As my financial situation deteriorated, I made an agreement with myself to stop buying and start being responsible with money. But establishing a hold over my finances took a back seat to just one more piece of furniture, another pair of shoes, or one last shrub for my garden.

When I did not keep an agreement, I neglected to hold myself accountable to stay true to my word. Yet, I am the one responsible for the agreements I make with myself and other people. Whatever excuses I created to defend my irresponsible actions were only my self-deceiving ego. Making excuses did not make me feel better about going against my word. Excuses do nothing to make people we let down trust us or depend on us to keep the promises we make going forward.

I do not overeat anymore. I exercise regularly, I no longer smoke, and I am financially responsible. What made the difference was realizing that each time I crossed my heart and told myself I was going to do something and then did not follow through, I was actually lying to myself. The same was true each time I told someone else an untruth, did not arrive at the time I promised, or chose not to do what I said I would. I learned that not saying what I meant and not keeping my word hurt me and other people too.

My mother was eight years old when a relative promised her a sherbet party. Mom's family was poor, and at the time she had no idea what sherbet was. But it made her feel special, and she was very excited. For the next several days, Mom waited with eager anticipation. The days turned into weeks. My mother began to wonder how long until the party. Weeks turned into months. Months turned into years. Somewhere in time my mother forgave the relative, but she did not forget the pain and disappointment of the broken promise.

While in a class on the importance of keeping our word, my mother shared this story. A few weeks later, the members of the class had a luncheon. When it was time for dessert, a hushed stillness came over the room. One member of the group went to the freezer. As she returned, carrying a towel covering the surprise, the group was reminded of my mother's story and the relative's broken promise. The dessert was uncovered, and to my mother's delight, there were three different flavors of sherbet for everyone. The group made certain my mother finally got her sherbet party, almost eighty years later.

Ego, the part of us that regards us as the center of all things, with little or no regard for others' beliefs or attitudes, will justify why we do not really have to keep our word. Ego will defend our right to be condescending and sarcastic. Ego tells us it is okay to be dishonest, especially if we can get away with it. Ego convinces us that keeping our word is overrated.

To lead with our heart we refuse to allow egocentric self-centeredness to rationalize or excuse irresponsible behavior.

When you and I make a promise, either to ourselves or to someone else, we love ourselves by making good on that promise. We also accept that it takes self-discipline to say no up front to requests for our help, time, skills, and other resources when we know we will not be able to fulfill the obligation or we just do not want to participate. In the long run, being respected for being honest and keeping our word is more important than being liked.

Having the heart to honestly evaluate ourselves brings us deep peace and personal satisfaction. Moving away from behaving carelessly and toward remaining aware of our actions and how they impact us, others, and all life is a result of the questions we ask—and the actions we take to better ourselves in response to the answers we receive.

Sincere assessment of ourselves and our behavior is the way to identify self-centered illusions, rationalizations, and excuses that are preventing us from seeing ways to avoid problems and create the relationships we want that make life meaningful.

Take a moment to examine the image below.

At first, the figure appears to be a simple configuration of twenty-five black blocks. After a few seconds, we notice ghost-like gray spots that appear at the inner corners of the squares.

The spots are not real. They are optical illusions, afterimages our mind creates.

The above figure with its ghostly gray spots illustrates the illusions or deceptions that arise when we allow a "my view is right" attitude to take the lead in forming the perceptions we have of ourselves, other people, and situations.

One of the first steps to leading with your heart is learning to remain aware of the deceptions a self-centered view creates. My ego created the misconception that the man on the interstate who was driving aggressively was totally at fault while I was completely innocent. In my exchange with the professor, my ego tricked me with the illusion that Dr. X was the one entirely at fault. He was the one who behaved inappropriately. Yet, when I broadened the limited view my ego's hurt pride had created, I realized that reacting to him a second time with inconsiderate behavior would not have gotten the results I really wanted. My ego was creating a fantasy, an illusion that telling him off would get him to see how badly he was behaving.

The act of stopping to consider how you want to remember your behavior in an exchange can shatter your ego's illusion that you have to defend yourself and prove others wrong. Looking at your side of any exchange will help you appreciate that you cannot egotistically fight fire with fire and expect not to get burned.

The experience of asking ourselves how we want to remember our behavior provides the incentive to walk away proud of ourselves. Being objective about our conduct also allows us to be grateful for the observations others have of us, rather than just shutting them out with the narrow, egocentric, defensive "I am right about me" angle.

It used to upset me when people pointed out things about my manners they thought were inappropriate. I did not welcome being told, "You do not listen. You are too impulsive. You are emotionally disconnected. You really need to think before you speak. You are irresponsible."

The nerve! Then one day my heart was open and I heard what was said. Honestly taking the comments into consideration resulted in a new realization: when I become uncomfortable with, or offended by, something someone says about me, or when someone challenges my actions, it is a red flag, a sign for me to look within.

Instead of getting angry and impulsively shooting the messenger, as I had in the past, I took to heart what was offered. With honest assessment, I recognized the behaviors pointed out about me were true. By responsibly questioning why my ego was pricked, I was able to accept other people's observations.

Taking their comments to heart, I began focusing on truly listening to other people. With practice I learned how to quiet my mind so I heard what was being said. I concentrated on keeping myself from interrupting or formulating a response while someone was still talking.

Teaching myself to remain connected to someone's words as they spoke also helped me learn to be a more patient person. I realized that when I am patient I am also present in the moment. When I am present in the moment I am connected to my heart and what I am feeling. And once I had the patience and awareness to think before speaking, it became easier to discern those who were making accurate observations about my behavior from those who just projected their shortcomings onto me.

Today, I work to remain aware of, and connected to, my words and conduct by listening as I want to be heard, speaking as I want to be spoken to, and treating other people as I want to be treated. Yet no matter how closely I pay attention to my thoughts, words, and actions, I am not perfect by a long shot—I never will be, and that's okay. Occasionally someone still points out something he or she sees about me that could be improved. I voluntarily take the advice. Now I recognize that one handy tool for identifying necessary change in myself is to listen to and appreciate the messenger.

By being open to what others say, we receive gifts in the form of answers and candid observations about ourselves that, if listened to, sincerely evaluated, and applied, will make us better people. And when we are better people, our relationships will be better.

Remember, deep, lasting, and intimate relationships are based on shared values that govern behavior. Patient people like to be around calm people. Compassionate people seek out those with big hearts. Honest people like truthful people. Self-disciplined people relate to other people who share their level of self-control. So courageously asking yourself hard questions, and sincerely wanting to find the answers, will help you determine the positive conduct you value, so you can exchange those behavior standards with others.

Don't be afraid to ask yourself hard questions and then honestly embrace the answers. Fear cannot grow where the light of truth shines. Having nothing to hide is true freedom.

MEDITATIONS AND EXERCISES

Sit down in a quiet place and write down your answers to these questions:

1. Do you keep the agreements you make to yourself and other people? Write down one incident when someone forgot or failed to stick to their promise. What were the circumstances? How did it feel? *No - going to the gym and I don't go* *for m pot*

2. Now, write down one incident when you forgot or failed to stick to your promise. What were the circumstances?

How did it feel? Have you ever said yes when you knew in your heart you should say no? How could you have avoided letting this person down?

3. When does your ego create challenges, miscommunication, and defensiveness in your relationships? How might that be avoided?

When the opportunity arises, try this exercise:

The relationships you have with others will not be perfect, but they will offer perfect opportunities to work on your imperfections. When someone makes a comment about your behavior, take a deep breath, count to five, and stop prideful ego (resentment, envy, anger, projection, hurt feelings, superiority, or inferiority) from automatically discounting what is being said. Listen with an open heart. Notice how differently these interactions turn out.

NOTES

Evaluate Rather than Judge

One time my uncle's car broke down on a sparsely populated stretch of two-lane highway. This happened long before cell phones, and he was stuck in the middle of nowhere. He had to depend on the off chance that someone would happen along.

After a while he heard a soft buzzing that sounded like a swarm of bees heading in his direction. As the noise grew louder, he watched the horizon. Soon a group of motorcycle riders crested the hill.

Even though my uncle had not personally encountered bikers before, he was terrified at the sight of them. He had formed a critical conclusion of motorcycle riders from others' opinions and harbored a preconceived idea that they were all dangerous. He feared they would rob and possibly harm him. With nowhere to hide, he felt completely helpless as he watched them approach.

I've known several tattooed biker guys with scraggly beards, do-rags, and wallets on chains, and I realize how they might seem ominous. Yet, I know from experience that we cannot accurately measure the true character of any person or group of people based on a stereotype.

Most of the motorcycle group waved as they passed by my uncle. Two riders stopped and politely asked if they could be of help. They discovered the problem and repaired it, and soon my uncle was back on the road with a new perspective on people who ride motorcycles.

Evaluation is the process of determining the true value of something based on evidence and reasoning. Heart evaluation works the same way. It involves investing time to gauge ourselves, the situation, and others from many different angles, with the goal of determining the truth for ourselves.

My uncle made a critical assessment, an ego judgment, based on little or no evidence. This isn't uncommon. Such opinions are often formed about those whose religion, ethnicity, political beliefs, or socioeconomic status is different from our own.

But remember that opinion is not fact. Opinion is: (1) a belief or judgment that rests on grounds insufficient to produce complete certainty, and (2) a personal view, attitude, or appraisal.

For instance, I am a positive person; but this does not mean my head is buried in the sand. It would be easy for me to develop a negative opinion of life if I based it only on news reports or the editorial commentary to which I am exposed. The reality is there are countless media sources that think nothing of altering images or even staging photos or making things up for impact. Even responsible media deliver news of depressing events right into our homes. Media bombard us with tragedy and the worst of human behavior. If we allow ourselves to latch on to the pessimistic representations of what is wrong with the world, then we would feel as if we were hopelessly surrounded by negative people and irreversible situations. We would automatically look at others with a judgmental eye.

For the past several years, a man and woman have been walking by my apartment building each day. I'd always supposed they were husband and wife going to lunch at a neighborhood restaurant. We'd frequently pass each other on the sidewalk, smile, and exchange hellos.

One morning I woke to find a flyer under my door with a photo of the man and a warning that he is a convicted sex offender. I saw that same flyer had been left at other homes on the street, as well as on the automobiles. Three things hit me at once.

First, this was a man I had seen for many years. Before allowing myself to go to the place of fear and condemnation, I went to the Internet. I found his public record and discovered many years ago he had abused two children under the age of sixteen, but he'd had no recent offenses or convictions.

Second, papering the neighborhood with this information seemed personal. While investigating this man, I found there were three other convicted sex offenders in the neighborhood. They had photos and similar offenses. None of those men living a block or two away was included in this notification. In addition, much of the information on the flyer, such as the car the man drove or the neighborhood places he frequented, was not available on his public record. It seemed that someone who knew him personally may have done this to deliberately humiliate him.

Third, yes, he was indeed someone of concern to the community. The man's prior convictions, coupled with the low rate of rehabilitation for sex offenders, raised the valid possibility that he may abuse again. But what if this man commits no further offenses? When do we stop identifying people with their mistakes? When do we accept that some people do change for the better? When do we forgive others as we want to be forgiven?

At eleven years old, I was molested by my babysitter. At seventeen, I was molested by a physician. I know how it feels to experience emotional, psychological, and physical pain because of the actions of others. Because of this, I will be the first to stand up and challenge the justifiability of someone who continues to be a threat to society having the same rights as a non-offender.

On the other hand, I have done many things in the past of which I am not proud. Over the years I've changed many, many things about myself. So much so that I am not the same person today that I was even a year ago. While I know I cannot expect everyone to forgive my past actions, I appreciate when people do, and I try to forgive others for their misdeeds, too.

Maybe those people from my past with less-than-pleasant memories of how I treated them will continue to see me as irresponsible and self-centered. Or maybe they will be open to allowing my current behavior to paint a more accurate picture of who I really am today, since the fact is I have changed.

While past behavior is frequently a good predictor of future actions, this belief cannot be automatically applied to everyone, in every instance. When we refuse to acknowledge that a person may have changed, it is an egotistical limitation. Too often we justify making up evidence to support our reasons for not giving someone the benefit of the doubt, even when their current behavior has turned in a positive direction. No matter what happened in the past, I am the first to support people who actually do change their behavior from negative to decidedly positive.

Accepting that people change is not forgetting or condoning what they did. It is not offering a free pass to people who have a history of criminal or abusive behavior so they can continue to act as they please. We do not allow people with a history of child sexual abuse to interact with children. But as in the case of the man in my neighborhood who, according to public record, has not reoffended in decades, evaluating facts allows us to recognize positive change in others by placing greater importance on an individual's current consistent behavior rather than continuing to judge and associate him or her with past actions.

When someone we know has a history of being an abuser or an angry, controlling, or irresponsible person, and that person replaces promises to change with concrete actions that result in new, consistently positive behavior, then he or she is taking the first steps toward changing for the better. The loving, faithful step we can take is learning to release the residual fear that results from enduring the person's past behavior.

Leading with your heart means dropping old images of what you and other people were like in the past. It means allowing the people in your life opportunities to create new histories of positive behavior. It means placing within your heart the awareness that people do change for the better.

Rather than jump to judgment, ask questions of yourself and others. Do your research. Evaluate and seek truth for yourself rather than blindly believing or spreading the opinions of others, or yourself. Seeking the facts, even about everyday issues you may consider minor, supports you in making the best decisions that avoid problems and make life easier for yourself and others.

One day my neighbor called to say that a woman who lives down the street was taking oranges off my trees. I am friendly with the woman and have encouraged her to pick them, so I was not upset—until I learned that in the process of gathering the fruit she had crushed many of the flowers I'd planted below. I went downstairs to find several broken plants.

Later in the week, the woman stopped me on the street. Before I could share my disappointment in finding so many crushed flowers, she spoke up.

"My five-year-old granddaughter insisted we take all the oranges I could reach. I lost my balance and stepped on your flowers. I am so sorry. I also want you to know the oranges were not for us. Every time my granddaughter visits me, she goes through my refrigerator for leftovers and my purse for loose change. Then we walk up the street and she gives them to the homeless man who sits in front of Peet's coffee shop. That day she wanted as many oranges as possible to give to him, too."

It took about three weeks for most of the flowers to recover. There was one bald patch. I thought of getting a few more plants to fill it in but decided against it. The spot served to remind me of the loving behavior of the young girl and that it is best not to jump to conclusions because others' actions are not necessarily what they might seem.

To create deep relationships, avoid problems, and make life easier, we accept that it is not responsible to jump to conclusions based on hearsay or prejudicial fear. Instead of buying into negativity or opinion, we care enough about ourselves and others to search for truth.

MEDITATIONS AND EXERCISES

Honest evaluation makes you heart-aware. With heart-awareness, you see yourself and the world more accurately, and in a more positive light.

Sit down in a quiet place and write down your answers to these questions:

1. Have you ever been on the receiving end of an untrue rumor or opinion? What were the circumstances? How did it make you feel? *Yes — work conflict, not good, at all*

2. How much negativity are you exposed to each day? Do *some* you notice any trends in where the negativity comes from? (Individuals? Locations? Time of day?)

3. Whom do you know who has decidedly changed for the better? Ask these people how they've accomplished it.

4. In what ways are you different from even a year ago? What positive lasting changes have you made?

I need to stop getting involved in gossip. Listen, but don't respond, I need to be in the present moment

Question Your Beliefs

The society in which I was raised believed the following:

- God is male, Jesus Christ is his true messenger, and Christianity is the only divinely sanctioned belief system; questioning the Bible in any way is blasphemous.
- Men are superior; women should be subservient.
- White people are better than people of color.
- Homosexuality is an intentional choice to sin against God.
- Animals are stupid and really do not have feelings.

When I was growing up, people expected me to adopt the same beliefs they held. Even as a young girl, I found attempting to accept such limited, disparaging ideas caused me such anxiety, suffering, and feelings of unworthiness and shame that I lived in constant fear. It felt as if I were slowly being crushed beneath the oppressive weight of powerlessness and hopelessness. I thought life was too painful to continue, but I did not give up. Instead, I questioned why much of what I was taught just did not feel right to my heart. Challenging the status quo of what we are taught takes courage and desire, and it's a crucial part of becoming an adult that we must all face at some point.

Questioning beliefs is imperative. The people who teach us beliefs, answer our questions, dole out punishment and reward, and mirror society's behaviors are passing along what they have learned or been exposed to. While they may have more experience than we do, that does not mean we should blindly accept what is passed on to us.

Take religious foundations, for example. These are some of

the most deeply rooted beliefs you will find. It was under a strict religious system that I was taught to follow what was accepted as the norm in order to fit in. By doing certain things I would get to go to heaven, and if I behaved in negative ways I would go to hell.

Only through assessment did I come to realize that had I adopted some of the beliefs I was taught, they would have prevented me from creating a joyful, peaceful, and responsible life. It was only through challenging myself to move past limitations and denigration that I was able to advance my spiritual and emotional intelligence.

Beliefs about God

I was brought up in a fundamentalist Christian church in Texas. I was taught God is angry, vengeful, and male. As a small child, God was scary and something to fear. But that did not make sense to my soul. So I decided to do my own research, because to me leaving limiting beliefs unexamined is really limiting God.

Regardless of what other people wanted me to believe, it made sense to me that if a supreme awareness initiated the events resulting in the creation of everything, then a part of that consciousness must reside in all human beings and in all that is alive.

This means that by design the original creative consciousness must have bestowed a spark of itself equally in both men and women. Judaism teaches that every person (Jewish and non-Jewish) was created *b'tzelem Elohim,* which is Hebrew for "in God's image." For this reason, every person is equally important and has an infinite potential to do good in the world.

One indication that this supreme consciousness was placed into male form by male authors and translators of the Christian Bible is found in the meaning of the word Jesus Christ used originally to address the Divine in the Lord's Prayer. According to the monk Michael Green,

> When Jesus lived he spoke Aramaic, an archaic language that frames matters of the Spirit more softly, and perhaps more appropriately, than the truncated Latin, German or English translations of the gospel that are now so much a part of our heritage. Biblical scholars inform us now that when the Son of Mary addressed the mystery of Godhead, the actual word Jesus used is ABWOOM, a term that has always been rendered for us as Our Father, but would be more properly understood as Our Mother-Father-All-in-All.

Jesus was not the first or last enlightened messenger who was careful about placing supreme consciousness into a particular form. Consider the following verses from the Upanishads, a collection of sacred Hindu texts addressing the relationship between our human and spiritual being and written centuries before the birth of Jesus Christ.

1

. . . That which makes the tongue speak but which cannot be spoken by the tongue—that alone is God, not what people worship.

That which makes the mind think but which cannot be thought by the mind—that alone is God, not what people worship.

That which makes the eye see but which cannot be seen by the eye—that alone is God, not what people worship.

That which makes the ear hear but which cannot be heard by the ear—that alone is God, not what people worship.

2

If you think you know God, you know very little; all that you can know are ideas and images of God.

I do not know God, nor can I say that I don't know It.

If you understand the meaning of "I neither know or I don't know," you understand God.

Those who realize that God cannot be known, truly know; those who claim that they know, know nothing.

The ignorant think that God can be grasped by the mind; the wise know It beyond knowledge. . . .

The Episcopal priest Barbara Brown Taylor agrees that we put limitations on ourselves by placing labels or particular forms on a divine being. She writes:

As a preacher, I spend most of my life pressed up against the limits of language. I do not have the foggiest idea of who God really is. I am not even sure I want to know, since any such knowledge would by definition blow all my existing circuits.

I hold a deep faith within my heart that an infinite loving power exists. To me, it is one who gives birth to all, or our divine parent, or Radiance who shines through all that is. I believe that it has no specific gender, race, or ethnicity. It does not exclusively endorse any one person, group of people, or particular set of religious beliefs. These all-inclusive, positive, life-affirming values allow me to honor the divine spark of it equally in each human being regardless of gender, race, social status, position within society, or spiritual practice. Inclusive acceptance also fosters a deep appreciation for, and obligation to honor and protect, all animals and the natural world.

Deliberately changing attitudes about the Divine, I believe, provides a more balanced and accurate view of the world. Seeing the divine spark in myself and others allows me to understand that the plan for human beings was not misogyny and patriarchy. Recognizing the value of everything alive is to value its overall design, and treat all people and life with reverence.

Once I refused to buy into the limiting belief that the divine source is male, I also stopped believing that Christianity was the only true path, or Jesus Christ the only enlightened messenger. Actually, the beliefs I was asked to adopt as a child were even more limiting. The particular denomination of the Church of Christ I attended was deemed to be the only true belief system sanctioned by God and His only son, Jesus. My father chose to attend the Episcopal church instead. What about him, or my Jewish, Catholic, and Buddhist friends? I was led to believe they were going to hell.

How it is possible to treat other people as I want to be treated if I believe a single path or its founding messenger is the only divinely sanctioned one? These beliefs discount that human-kind's peaceful and purposeful practices are designed to connect us with a consciousness greater than ourselves. The fundamental essence of spirituality, to establish a relationship with the Divine so our relationships with other people and all life changes for the better, neither began nor ended with Christianity and the man/heart called Jesus.

By doing my own research, I learned the belief systems of Native American and Australian Aboriginal peoples go back much farther than Hinduism, which originated approximately two thousand years before the birth of Christ. Many of the world's major religions, including Judaism, Buddhism, Taoism, and Confucianism, were created well before Christianity. Islam and Sikhism were founded after Christianity.

These religions originated with men in times when women had little or no status within their societies. The peacefully motivated founders of the major religions challenged all human beings to move past a controlling, self-centered, ego-thought identification and live by a higher, responsible internal wisdom, such as the Native American peoples' deep respect for the natural world, or the Hindu ideals of nonviolence, truthfulness, friendship, compassion, fortitude, self-control, purity, and generosity.

It did not feel right in my heart to be forced to adopt a right/wrong, fearful, or proprietary view of spirituality. While I deeply cherish Jesus, I also equally honor the peaceful, life-enhancing behavior of all messengers of enlightenment. Today, both male and female representatives of our best potential continue to walk together with us, offering keys to joy, accountability, and peace.

The goal is for human beings to intimately connect with one another and live guided by their hearts. Regardless of what path is chosen, living a peaceful, nonjudgmental life is proof that the messages of compassion, equality, accountability, and kindness have been permanently written on our heart. It does not matter what name was/is assigned to the messenger.

Was it blasphemous for me to question what I was taught to believe? No. It was, and continues to be, spiritually responsible to consider my faith.

Beliefs about Men and Women

The women in my life taught me to bow to the wishes of men. I was told to lose at sports on purpose so that boys could feel good about themselves. I was taught they would like me if I reinforced how much better they were than me. I was expected to silently wait on men hand and foot.

As I questioned what I was taught to believe, I discovered the purposeful division between genders had ancient roots. According to author Leonard Shlain:

Millennia ago males intentionally set themselves above females when they realized women were the only ones capable of birthing new life. Today we continue to live under patriarchal societies with sets of institutionalized social rules put in place by men to control the sexual and reproductive rights of women.

The resulting widespread disdain for women and belittlement of the values commonly associated with the feminine have a long history in many of the world religions that were founded by men in times when women had no power. In *Sex, Time and Power,* Shlain observes:

The history of Christianity, Islam and Taoism darkly demonstrates that the religions that flowed from the teachings of Jesus, Muhammad and Lao Tzu have been most unkind to women. In every case, after the death of the founder, men with harsh patriarchal leanings seized the reins of power and revised whatever gentle counsel the originators of these traditions may have had to impart about women.

Angry and frustrated with both men and women, I spent much time questioning why we do not appreciate, honor, and support each other as equals. Through experience and examination of the world, I came to believe one reason is the continued widespread religious labeling of supreme consciousness as male.

Labels separate, elevate, ostracize, and judge. Human ego is quick to box something into its limited interpretation by placing a specific identity upon it. As soon as a label is placed on something or someone, our egocentric arrogance latches on to it. This limits us from being open to see any other possibility, even if the label perpetuates the abuse of power over others with discrimination, domination, suffering, and pain.

Believing a supreme consciousness is in both genders equally,

I no longer resent men or dislike being a woman, and I no longer allow myself to be treated as less-than by anyone. As I surround myself with men and women who value an equal division of labor and evenly balanced responsibilities in the home, I witness the tremendous difference it makes to the esteem of both girls and boys who have fathers and mothers who are equally emotionally present with child-rearing. Confident and responsible children develop as a result of parents who believe being gentle with themselves, other people, and other forms of life is one of the strongest things they can do.

Beliefs about Race

When I was four or five, my mom took me to her friend's house on Halloween. My sister and I were dressed in little scary outfits. We rang the doorbell and Mrs. Lilly, an older woman, answered. We said, "Trick or treat!" She smiled and put several pieces of candy into our bags.

As she was ushering us inside for a visit, a car pulled up to the curb. I looked back to see a little black girl, my age and dressed as a witch, stepping out of the car. Mrs. Lilly screamed, "Get back in that car, nigger. I do not want you coming up here. Go home where you belong."

There were tears streaming down the little girl's face as she got back into the car, and it's an image I will never forget. I sat in stunned silence as Mrs. Lilly returned her attention to my sister and me as if nothing had happened. For the rest of the evening I had a big lump in my throat.

In my heart of hearts, it did not feel right to believe I was better than other people because of my skin color. Many of my classmates were African-American and Hispanic. They were good-natured, we had lots in common, and I liked them. When we scraped our knees, our blood was the same color. We got hurt and our tears were the same. When it rained and we had to stay indoors all day, we shared the same disappointment. We all got sick with colds and the flu. We got hungry. We were sad, and cheerful, too. In my heart I knew we were similar, just with different colored skin.

Scientific research confirms modern humans are descendants of the same common ancestors who originated in Africa and were as dark-skinned as Africans are today. Our skin color began to lighten as our ancestors moved north into colder climates, an evolutionary change necessary for humans to maximize the synthesis of vitamin D.

We are a beautiful rainbow of colors and cultures, different branches of the same family tree. My skin color does not make me better than anyone else. Leading with my heart, I look beyond a person's outer physical appearance for the consistent positive behavior that reveals his or her true character.

Beliefs about Homosexuality

From the first time I stepped into a church, I was taught to believe I was going to hell. What a lonely, depressing, and negative thing to ask someone to believe—especially a child. Although no one had a clue about me, I was surrounded by people who believed their God hated me for being gay. They felt justified in hating me, too.

With absolutely no one to talk with, not even a divine source, I was all alone. There was no person with whom it was safe to share the pain, confusion, and despair of being harshly and falsely condemned. The frustrating part was that I did not deliberately choose to sin against their God. I was born this way.

This judgment did not make sense in my heart of hearts. Even as a young child I questioned how, when the basic message of all faith is to "treat others as you want to be treated," could I not be worthy? It did not make sense that spirituality was intended to be an exclusive, criteria-based membership, a contest of me against other people, or a practice based on fearing some unseen angry and condemnatory presence. Isn't spirituality the individual quest to connect with and behave motivated by the spark of goodness within my heart? Didn't that mean supporting others as I want to be supported, loving as I want to be loved, and being the best person possible?

Being gay is not a punishment from a divine source. It is not a conscious choice a child makes. Doctors, psychiatrists, psychologists, and educators have all concluded sexual orientation is not a choice. Although there is no simple single cause for sexual orientation, research suggests it is a combination of genetic, hormonal, and environmental influences. Psychiatrist and author Jeffrey Satinover, MD, concludes:

> *Like all complex behavioral and mental states, homosexuality is neither exclusively biological nor exclusively psychological, but results from an as-yet-difficult-to-quantitate mixture of genetic factors, intrauterine influences, postnatal environment (such as parent, sibling and cultural behavior), and a complex series of repeatedly reinforced choices occurring at critical phases of development.*

As far as religious references, only six or seven of the one million–plus verses in the Bible address same-sex relationships. None of those verses refers to homosexual orientation as it is understood today.

Modern biblical scholars advise us that the verses regarding same-sex relationships, and others throughout ancient religious texts, need to be understood within the context of the societies which produced them. One of those scholars is Reverend Mel White, PhD, Christian minister, author, filmmaker, and cofounder of SoulForce. He writes:

Over the centuries the Holy Spirit has taught us that certain Bible verses should not be understood as God's law for all time periods. Some verses are specific to the culture and time they were written, and are no longer viewed as appropriate, wise, or just. Often, the Holy Spirit uses science to teach us why those ancient words no longer apply to our modern times.

Too often we believe religious texts are not to be challenged. But as someone who was born gay and who realized at a very young age that I was different, I had to challenge the Bible and the judgmental discrimination I was being taught about myself if I was going to survive.

The truth is, I did try to change to be "normal." And I suffered more. So I either had to live a lie by going against myself to be what other people said was right or I had to choose to live an honest life by remaining true to who I was born to be. The bottom line is that even if being gay would have been my choice, we must question how responsible it is to use particular verses to rationalize the condemnation of those whose sexuality, religion, ethnicity, political beliefs, and socioeconomic status are different from our own. History repeatedly shows us that war, suffering, slavery, and the abuse of women, animals, and our planet, as well as divisive beliefs, result from misusing the Bible and other religious texts. Questioning limited and harsh beliefs, including those against homosexuality, is spiritually prudent, particularly since science now provides evidence for biological and environmental causes. Therefore, it is spiritually responsible to evaluate someone's good character not by their sexual orientation, but rather by how responsibly he or she behaves.

Emerging on the other side of such a painful journey, I learned it is not possible to judge and love at the same time. Judgment is egocentric. Love is of heart. The divine power I believe in manifests itself as love. That power loved me and did not condemn me for being born the way I am. Leading with my heart, I strive to be an accepting person, treating other people as I want to be treated.

Beliefs about Animals

Today, I also thank the Divine for my gentle, unconditional love and acceptance of animals. In truth, much of the credit for helping save my life goes to animals.

Growing up alone under the heaviness of persecution caused me to retreat into a solitary world filled with animals, the natural world, and imaginary friends. I became close to and protective of my furry friends, the only ones who loved me unconditionally. They were the ones I could talk to, which often made it difficult to obey orders to leave our dog outside during a thunderstorm.

Our big golden lab, Caesar, was terrified during a storm. He threw himself against the garage door or cowered in his doghouse and made pitiful sounds. It broke my heart to see him afraid. I respected how it felt to be frightened, with nowhere to hide and no one to comfort him.

The belief that other animals (human beings are animals too) are stupid and without feelings is an emotionally distancing and arrogant ego-illusion. While I accept dogs and other animals do not reason to the extent human beings do, they *do* still reason and they do suffer. Like us, other animals feel hunger, pain, thirst, fear, affection, joy, and loneliness. They become tired, cold, hot, and scared. They welcome respect, patience, and kindness just as we do. Caring for and respecting all animals and the natural world is a spiritual responsibility. This is essential if we are to genuinely care for and respect the divine power we believe in.

Questioning Beliefs Allows Us to Advance

If we are going to create lives of love, compassion, and purpose, we have the charge to question what we believe. It is only by asking questions of ourselves and the world that we can improve from generation to generation.

Imagine life without the vast medical advancements of the past couple hundred years. Research and evaluation are how theories and formulas are adapted, adjusted, made more reliable and applicable, or wisely abandoned.

At first we thought the atom was the smallest particle of matter. Then we discovered even smaller particles: electrons, protons, and neutrons. And with particle accelerators, we discovered smaller things yet, called quarks.

Until the mid-twentieth century, we had no idea of the vastness of outer space. Then we discovered the Earth resides in a galaxy among billions of others.

We are part of a continuous chain of asking questions and wanting answers. We come to conclusions and pass them on to the next generation. Advancing the complexity of the questions we ask, and making positive adjustments based on our findings, is a part of the natural process of change.

Everything is designed to change and progress—the seasons, our planet, nature; scientific, technological, and cosmological discoveries; even ourselves. This means our spiritual beliefs, texts, and practices are designed to change and advance as well. We have the duty to grow our heart at a rate that surpasses our technological growth. Spiritual advancement ensures we bring accountability, forethought, compassion, equality, and principled excellence to the table when addressing challenges and opportunities.

No matter what is written in ancient texts, we can change what is deemed spiritually responsible as our world changes.

Pushing against the status quo is exactly what each enlightened messenger has done and continues to do. We are being asked to do the same.

Expressing our heart nature is asking hard questions and addressing tender issues. As environmental activists, animal advocates, and lovers of the natural world, we stand up to those who do not think twice about destroying our planet for monetary gain. We represent peace instead of conflict, cooperation instead of division, conscientiousness instead of carelessness, and empathy instead of cruelty. We stand on the unselfish side of humanity, devoting ourselves to leaving the world a better place for our having lived.

We question the spiritual correctness of encouraging irresponsible population growth when this is a top environmental concern human beings face. We do not ignore dwindling natural resources and the impact of human population on our delicate ecosystem. We have created oceans full of trash and are rapidly decreasing marine life. We have polluted our rivers and waterways. We have polluted our Earth. We are a make-it, break-it, throw-it-away world. These irresponsible behaviors align not with people who actively lead with their heart, but with those who lead with ego.

Of course, it would be impossible to find a direct reference in ancient religious texts dealing with the negative results of modern technological and industrial advancements—but that does not mean we are not responsible. In my heart, I do not think there will be a time in the future when one form of higher consciousness arrives, or returns, and causes us to be transformed. There is not one entity outside of us that will come back and make us instantly responsible for our actions, or motivate us to come together as a human family to finally live in peace.

Consciousness messengers did not leave us. Enlightened

teachers continue to share with us that goal for us to transcend ego and live as self-aware beings who lead with heart. The consistent message of our teachers is to consciously behave in ways that create the peace and joy we want right now. Consequently, we are the ones we are waiting for, as only the mindful, positive actions you and I take today will result in a peaceful world tomorrow.

The time has come to stop egocentrically judging one another over religion. It is time to lead with our heart and develop a spiritual practice that motivates us to behave from our heart. The goal is for us to tap into the highest, wisest part of ourselves by deepening our connection to and compassion for other people, all animals, and the natural world. The time has come for us to move past focusing on our differences, especially in the important area of spirituality in our lives. Because until we have the courage to question the belief that we are somehow better than other people, other animals, or other faiths, we will continue to see the world and others through our egocentric mind, not our loving heart.

Let's encourage each other to practice any spiritual path that results in our living as nonviolent, responsible, respectful, supportive, peaceful, and positive people. Let's courageously and freely open ourselves to the truth that our practice, awareness, and writings of spirituality are designed to change and progress as a result of the questions we ask that push the boundaries of restrictive, divisive, and condemnatory beliefs. Let us realize that if we are offended by or afraid of this, then we accept responsibility for allowing our egocentric, fearful mind to limit the intended advancement of our heart.

Whether we're talking about religion, politics, other cultures, animals, or ideas we have about ourselves, we must question what we believe. Question your exposure to news media, television, movies, the Internet, and the opinions of others. Examine your beliefs about a supreme consciousness. Challenge ancient religious texts and any rule that dictates fearful, derogatory, limiting, or oppressive behavior.

Just because we have been taught to believe something does not necessarily make it true. Likewise, just because we are taught *not* to believe something does not necessarily make it false. Make the choice to lead with your higher wisdom and take charge of courageously questioning beliefs that do not align with the positive, loving, inclusive behaviors of your heart.

MEDITATIONS AND EXERCISES

Sit down in a quiet place and write down your answers to these questions:

1. What beliefs cause you fear, stress, self-hatred, or judgment of yourself and others?

2. Do you experience equality between genders in your home, workplace, church, and community? Why do you think this is or is not the case?

3. How many of your friends belong to a different race, religion, or culture from yours? Ask them to tell you about their culture or religion.

4. Are you gay, or do you have any friends or family members who are gay? Do you think gay people should have the same rights as heterosexuals? Describe your feelings about this.

5. Do you have a pet? Do you think that animals have feelings? What have you done to respect wildlife and to promote the humane treatment of animals?

NOTES

Lead with Your Heart

Face Your Fear

There was a time in life when I lived in fear. I was scared of dying, of getting cancer, of success, of failure. I was afraid of going to hell, of not being liked, of being alone.

Today, I can honestly say I no longer live in fear. That's not to say I do not become afraid at times. At 3:00 a.m. when an earthquake jolts me awake, yes, absolutely, my heart races and my palms sweat as my fight-or-flight response kicks in. But I have learned that living in fear based on the negativity I am exposed to, or the trepidations of my creative and anxious mind, is no way to live.

Our mind thinks it is the wise one and will adamantly defend what it believes to be true and best. But within our mind's efforts of self-preservation also lies that distressing emotion of fear that distances us from our positive emotions and other people, and it prevents us from striving to live our best life.

Our mind is not the faithful part of us, no matter how loudly and persistently it tells us it is. Through a lifetime of experience, I learned it is our responsible, caring, and loving heart that is the higher, wiser, faith-filled part. We discover this by bravely doing the very things our mind tells us to be fearful of. By courageously facing each of our fears, we start walking in faith, both in a power greater than ourselves, and also in our ability to deal positively with life, regardless of what may come along.

For example, when doctors found a golf ball–size tumor in my partner's right kidney, they told her the diagnosis was renal cell carcinoma. Often these tumors are malignant. A biopsy cannot be performed, since the test itself causes the cancer to spread outside the kidney.

When she told me, my mind instantly wanted to rush to the place of fear. My thoughts told me I had to worry. But after taking a deep breath and pausing to get control of my fearful mind, my response was, "Okay, what do we need to do?" I did not allow myself to panic or be anxious about the future.

Taking time to settle back into the present moment, I remained connected to the truth that worry only spawns the anxiety, stress, and impatience that come from the notion that I am able to control the uncontrollable. Fear does not help us know the unknowable, change the unchangeable, or prevent the unpreventable. Accepting that we are powerless to prevent, change, foresee the outcome of, or control certain situations requires us to have faith. We walk in faith by remaining focused on our ability to successfully get through the situations in life where we are powerless to effect the change we want.

My partner quickly had surgery to remove her kidney. The tumor was malignant. She is now cancer-free, because the tumor was completely encased within her kidney.

We're frequently faced with situations where our ability to make a tangible impact on the outcome eludes us. We may be unexpectedly downsized, diagnosed with an illness, or learn our tax return is being audited. We may hear a family member has been battling an addiction, or we might return from shopping to find our car's been stolen.

We can choose to face the challenges of life with fear, anger, worry, or stubborn attempts to control the uncontrollable. But stop to think about it for a minute. Fear does not help us prepare for a tax audit. Anxiety does not allow us to think clearly about how best to look for a new job. Dread does not empower us to support someone through their recovery. Panic does not make loss easier to deal with. Our loved ones need us to be supportive, calm, and reassuring when facing tough situations, not anxious and sullen.

Replacing fear with positive action is the best way to support ourselves and those who need us. We have faith by choosing to use the anxiety we feel as a constructive motivator. Faith inspires us to accept those situations we cannot change. And in the situations where we do have control, self-confidence supports our actively creating change.

At one time, I worked for a shady organization. I caught my boss stealing money from a fundraising event that I had designed but he had taken the credit for. He was also accused of sexually assaulting a fellow employee, plus a variety of other offenses. Management refused to address the issues because the higher-ups were guilty of the same things.

Each day it became more difficult for me to go to work. My heart actually hurt when I walked into the office. One day I could not stand it anymore. No matter how much I needed the money, I refused to sell myself short any longer. The moment I decided to quit, some wonderfully positive energy seemed to align itself with me. Within a month, a great position working with good people came along. The energy I put out attracted similar energy.

Once I had transitioned out of the bad job, I realized that my sense of powerlessness and fear had been generated by thinking I had to keep that horrible job. The moment I released the dread of not knowing what I would do to get a new source of income, something beyond my power began to work on my behalf.

If you are stuck in a negative situation, sit down in a quiet place and honestly ask yourself what you really want. If you're like most people, as soon as you articulate what you want, an excuse for why you can't have it will pop up next. Release that apprehension of not knowing exactly how you will reach your goal. Remain focused. If fear returns, instead of allowing negative dread to consume you, take one action toward improving your situation. Keep moving forward in faith, and patiently watch for the opening of a new door. Then courageously walk through. Have faith that the optimistic energy you put out will come back to you. The longer you stay in any negative situation, whether it is a bad job or an abusive relationship, the more you break your heart. Nothing is worth that.

Self-confidence and strength are absolutely vital to prevent the things we can and to positively get to the other side of the problems in life that we create. There was a time it felt as if I were carrying the weight of the world on my shoulders. I had recently been laid off and was deeply in debt. Money difficulties and job loss were then complicated by a relationship breakup and the physical challenge of recovering from two major back-to-back spine surgeries.

It seemed anything that could go wrong had. Yet, deep within the honesty of my heart, I knew it was time to face the truth about my current situation. It was hard to admit I was responsible for getting myself into each of these challenging situations—even the back problem. The joy and peace I longed for were not possible until I did my best to put each of these struggles behind me. The only way to free myself of the numerous heavy loads was to stop running from them and finally face them head on.

Through self-assessment, I realized it was not possible to completely mend my back. For too many years, I'd stubbornly moved things much too heavy for my size and strength and ignored the sound advice to protect my spine with a brace or to ask for help. I was a natural athlete on the softball diamond and tennis court. That meant nothing when my 125-pound body met a sleeper sofa, a large boulder from a flower bed, or the oversized speakers and monitors I moved for years as a drummer in a rock band.

To most positively deal with the problem of what I had done to my body, I released the distress by honestly facing the fact that I would not be the same again physically. I surrendered to the reality of having to walk with a slight limp, of no longer spending hours bent over a flower bed, and of passing up requests from friends to help them move. I made an agreement with myself to protect my back by wearing a brace, asking for help, and exercising regularly to keep myself as flexible and strong as possible.

The weight of job loss hit me hard. Although I performed well, my management position was eliminated. I had worried for several months that a change was coming, but I did absolutely nothing to look for another position. Downsized with a master's degree and years of successful executive experience, I was certain I would find another position within a few months tops. The reality turned out to be much different. I searched for more than a year and a half before a position came along.

Now I faced a huge financial challenge. Accepting the truth caused such a deep panic I remember falling to the floor at the sheer impact of my situation. I was immediately filled with dread and worry. I could not imagine how I was going to pay off all my debts.

Worry did not magically generate a new job or a winning lottery ticket, and eventually I began letting go of unproductive fear and stress by accepting the reality that it was going to take much longer than I'd anticipated to find a job. The fear of what might happen was released when I began actively looking for a position daily, throughout the country and even internationally. When I was not sending out résumés or interviewing, I spent time volunteering, helping my family, reclaiming my body from the surgeries, and working with a lawn-mowing crew. I was the person who picked up cigarette butts and trash before they mowed. Since I smoked for so many years, this seemed a fitting way to ease the guilt I carried from decades of irresponsibly throwing out cigarette butts.

While the trash job offered a small income, being officially unemployed did not really help my financial situation. Without the sizeable income I had become accustomed to, I was forced to sell the new home I had built less than two years earlier. As I watched the last of my belongings being loaded into the moving van, I realized all this stuff did not ever make me content.

The tremendous problem of debt was the direct result of my spending with reckless abandon. Surrounding myself with things without considering how I would pay for them was a hollow attempt to fill some need I had. Maybe I needed the world to identify me as successful. Maybe I was trying to fill a hole in my heart left by a confusing childhood. Regardless of what I rationalized, I never saw the day when my purchases made me feel validated.

It took years to release the problem of financial recklessness. To get past the fear of such overwhelming debt I had to make a plan to become debt-free and then remain devoted to achieving that goal. I cut up every credit card, established a payback plan, stopped buying "stuff," and began filling the empty spaces within my heart, and the need for outside validation, with the self-love and acceptance that come from being responsible.

The same self-evaluation and proactive approach was necessary for me to move past the fear that I would continue to have unsatisfactory relationships. I realized I did not know what a good relationship was. On the other hand, I did know quite a lot about unhealthy relationships, since I had spent the majority of my life in them.

To move past the fear of being alone, and to break the pattern of having poor relationships, I accepted myself as the commonality. The faces of the people I'd dated looked different, but until I identified myself as the common denominator I continued attempting to get the other person to change. They did not, so I had to.

By establishing a loving, supportive, honest, and fulfilling relationship with myself, I dealt with my fear of continuing to have unsatisfactory relationships. Experience proved over and over again that my being insecure had never resulted in a positive relationship. And the joining of two self-doubting people only compounded the result, creating more dissatisfaction, blame, and negative discourse. I had to be self-sufficient, contented, and balanced before I could attract someone who had the same qualities. This was a key breakthrough: whatever you want in a relationship has to first be in you.

Over the course of my life, these are a few of the problems I created that resulted in tremendous amounts of self-induced fear. For too many years I ran from negative situations by thinking if I ignored them they would go away. But they never did. The more I passed the buck of responsibility for what I'd done to create the messes I found myself in, the larger the anxiety and dread became. It was not possible for me to have peace until I turned around and faced each of my problems head on.

Nothing positive comes from running away from the problems we create. Trying to shun responsibility or waiting for someone to come to our rescue only results in disappointment and heartache. The freedom and peace of mind we desire come from facing our problems with the faith that we can overcome the challenge of debt, unsatisfactory relationships, or even anger with a rude driver.

The goal is to stop creating fearful situations by making good choices in situations we can influence, such as those dealing with personal finances or health. We let go of fear by taking action to ensure we remain on top of business and financial obligations.

We lock our car, have regular health check-ups, and save for unexpected expenses. In all of our relationships, instead of fearing loss, we do our best to leave nothing we want to say unsaid. We give hugs, apologies, jokes, and forgiveness without hesitation. Each day we do everything within our power to better our life, the lives of those people we care about, and all living things.

Having the most peaceful and fulfilling life requires us to do our best to leave no room for the distress that comes from regret. We stay emotionally present and spend time with who and what we love. We listen attentively and say everything we want and need to, because life changes in a heartbeat. Life does not just change for other people; challenges will, in some way or another, happen to us, too. Maybe a tornado will take what we care for. Perhaps a fire, a job loss, or the death of a loved one will be the event that throws us a major curve.

We are not meant to live without challenges. We are meant to rise above to treasure who and what we love. When we leave no room for regret, challenge and loss become easier to accept, because we have embraced the pleasant memories while allowing ourselves to grieve and continue onward.

Leading with our heart requires replacing fear with faith. It means releasing the desire to control situations or people, or see the future, or change a past event. We accept our personal power by purposefully leaving no loose ends, so we move from day to day without regret. We allow the next moment to unfold as it will. We have faith in our ability to deal positively with life as it is, as it comes. Having faith is also relying on our belief in a power greater than ourselves to lift us up in times of challenge.

MEDITATIONS AND EXERCISES

Sit down in a quiet place and write down your answers to these questions:

1. What are some things that cause you to feel dread or apprehension?

2. What do you regret?

3. What steps can you take to replace fear with self-confidence and deal positively with life as it is and as it comes?

4. What problems do you want to release? Make a list of the actions you can take that will facilitate doing this.

--- NOTES ---

Start to
Think Differently

Honestly assessing your behavior, judgments, beliefs, and fears in Step One gave you a glimpse into how your thoughts create your behavior. Step Two challenges you to think differently, because the transformational force behind any positive change is a conscious change in thinking.

For instance, when I quit smoking I had to change my thinking from "it's okay to just have one cigarette" to "I am now a non-smoker who does not smoke even one." To stop ego-boxing I had to change my thinking from "I must defend myself against the rude behavior of others" to "I refuse to allow another person's actions to determine how I act." To stop placing greater value on the opinions of others to determine my worth, I had to change my thinking from "I need other people to tell me how good I am" to "I know that I am worthy and valid—and I don't need anyone else to confirm this." By thinking differently, my heart moved me past ego's need to be validated by others or to defend its self-centered behavior.

In this section, you'll release the idea that you need to be proven right so you can value your relationships with others over your need to feel superior. Accepting life as it is, you'll release the incorrect notion you can control what really cannot be controlled, or change what cannot be changed. Establishing how you want to be treated provides you with the self-loving and respectful thoughts necessary to create healthy boundaries in your relationships.

Learning to hear, trust, and act upon your heart's wise inner knowing is invaluable in helping you distinguish positive thoughts from those that are fear-based. When you determine your own criteria for success, the idea that you are only successful when you live up to the standards of others falls away. Conducting a candid inventory of what values make up, or are missing from, your character changes your beliefs about how best to create a loving, compassionate, and purposeful life.

When you change your thinking, your behavior changes. When your behavior changes, your life changes. This means it is necessary to continuously challenge your limiting thoughts to allow your heart's wise guidance to lead.

Let Go of the Need to Be Right

Through e-mail, I agreed to pick up and return my friend Katherine to the airport. Two weeks before her arrival, something came up that required me to change plans for transporting her back to the airport. Still through e-mail, I assured her I would find someone to give her a ride back.

She arrived and I was there to greet her. After some time together, I confirmed I was unable to give her a ride back to the airport. The news came as a shock. Nothing I said could convince my friend that I had sent a second e-mail two weeks earlier; she thought I was lying.

I can be stubborn, and I can be argumentative. But for too many years being obstinate and confrontational did nothing to resolve my conflicts. And clinging to the notion that I had to be proven right only added fuel to the fire in the disagreements I had with others. Through experience I learned the most positive action was choosing to overrule my self-centered ego.

It was not easy, but the truth was that no matter how much I wanted validation from Katherine, there was absolutely nothing to be gained by arguing with her. Leading with the heart is caring more for friendship than pride, so I chose to let go of my ego's need to be recognized as right. I did not want to be angry with her, nor did I want our time together to be uncomfortable. The only option I saw to ensure peace of mind was to be patient, accept what was, and allow the situation to resolve itself.

A few weeks after my friend returned home, she was having repairs made to her computer when several mysteriously lost e-mails arrived in her in-box. Among them was the one I had sent.

I do not believe it is possible for us to agree with everyone all the time about everything. I do believe it is possible for us to stay agreeable when disagreeing. And simply because we disagree with someone does not mean that person is wrong.

My friend was also right! She had not received my e-mail before she left. Yet, for many months after returning home, she was distant. She was embarrassed for not giving me the benefit of the doubt. She was upset at herself for allowing hurt feelings to invent all sorts of reasons to justify turning her back on me. She was also angry at herself for discounting my history of honest and loyal behavior. She was frustrated for permitting herself to invent ego-illusions that my innocent actions were a personal attack.

In the overall design, you and I are only alive for a very brief period—much too short to waste time holding a grudge or settling for drama, fear, and sadness. When we place more importance on being proven right than we do on our relationships, we have, in essence, donned flowing silk robes and placed ourselves in the middle of a dense rose garden. Life situations and interactions with other people become masses of twisted thorns that rip and tear at the fragile material. No matter how painful the thorns are or how deeply they tear at us, we are uncomfortable shedding the robe of our prideful self-image. Without our ego-centric self-view, who will we be?

With pride at stake, we do not stop to question the cost of being right. An egocentric mind does not care about the feelings of friends, family, or strangers. Wounded ego is not content unless the whole world accepts we are indeed right and someone else is wrong. And on the occasions we are the one who is wrong, our ego is not interested in voluntarily confessing our guilt; we are fine remaining quiet as a mouse sneaking off with a piece of cheese.

To lead with our heart, we let go of the need to be acknowledged as right—even when we are. While there may be two sides to every story, there is only one truth between them. Truth has a way of surfacing eventually, making relationships worth much more than egotistically defending our personal pride.

MEDITATIONS AND EXERCISES

Sit down in a quiet place and write down your answers to these questions:

1. Have you ever allowed the need to be right negatively impact your relationships? Describe how the situation arose and why you insisted that you were right. Upon reflection, was that the best course? How would you handle the situation now?

2. Can you think of a time when you and another person were both right? How was that situation resolved? What did you learn from the experience?

3. It's easy to distance oneself when conflict or a disagreement arise. If you've ever done this, describe the situation. What would have happened if you had given the other person the benefit of the doubt?

Lead with Your Heart

Accept What Is

On the way home to Birmingham, Alabama, from a vacation in Florida, we encountered a major traffic jam. Cars were bumper to bumper for miles. We inched along for more than two hours. With the slow passing of each mile I grew more impatient and more angry. *Why does this have to happen to me? How much longer do I have to be inconvenienced? Why is it taking so long to correct whatever the problem is?* By focusing on what I thought the situation should be, rather than accepting the truth of what it was, I caused a pleasant vacation to end badly.

After two months at a job selling advertising for a small, family-owned newspaper, I was fired. There was no warning. There was no indication my performance was less than acceptable. In fact, I had received praise for increasing ad revenue. It did not make sense that I was abruptly terminated. Regardless of how much I wanted to identify the reason, no one in the company returned my calls. I became angry and depressed. My attempts to determine what I should or could have done differently to prevent my dismissal only resulted in stress and frustration. Without accepting the reality that sometimes things happen with no logical explanation, I was stuck, unable to move on. For the next few months I did little to find a new job.

Many years ago, I dated an alcoholic. I did not recognize the condition in the beginning, but over time it became clear as the incidents of intoxication began to add up. After each occurrence there was an apology, a request for forgiveness, and a promise it would not happen again. No matter how much I wanted the drinking to stop, it did not. No matter how much I prayed for follow-through on the promise to seek help, there was none. For too long I chose to believe what was promised, rather than accepting the repeated actions as proof of what was actually true.

I once knew a man who thought he was in love with a friend of mine. Since a group of us spent time together going places, I knew she regarded him only as a friend. One day he shared with her the extent of his affection. The woman told him his friendship was valued, but she was engaged and devoted to a man who was serving in the military overseas. Instead of doing the loving thing and honoring her committed relationship, the man became obsessed with winning her heart and was determined to steal her from the man she loved. He sent flowers and gifts and repeatedly asked her out. He called her at all hours of the day and night and showed up at her door without notice. He refused to accept no for an answer. The man's escalating harassment left my friend no choice but to seek legal action.

A family I am acquainted with lost a teenage son to a tragic automobile accident. Before the accident, the father was a pillar of strength. He was also kind, compassionate, and had a positive outlook on life. That changed with the death of his son. Over the next few years he sank deeper into depression, clinging to what he thought should, would, or could have been. Blame was cast, lawsuits were filed, and a focus on revenge erased the memories of his once joyful life. Without the ability to forgive and deal with the tragedy, he was not able to be thankful for the joy life still held for him. He stopped caring about life or his health and eventually died a frail and bitter man.

How much precious time do you and I waste wanting other people or situations to be different from how they are? To lead with our heart, we must honestly look at how unreasonable it is to suffer under the false impression we have the power to control or change other people or the negative, frustrating, inconvenient, or heartbreaking situations we encounter in life. We are only able to control our response to them.

Life will not be without heartache. Maybe someone leaves us

for another or just ends the relationship. We have two choices. We can be angry, dwelling on what we think should be but isn't. Or we can mend our heart by learning from the experience, feeling our sadness, and picking ourselves up to move on. We choose to exchange a fantasy of the past and what "should be" for the opportunity to create a better "what is" reality in the present. This same formula works with whatever situations life throws at us.

Traffic jams and other delays are a frequent part of life. You and I do not receive the job we badly want and need. We realize we are in relationship with an abuser. We become conscious we are the one with a problem. The people and pets we love are sometimes taken away from us through illnesses or tragic accidents.

Relationships end. Our affection for another is not reciprocated. We slip and break an ankle. Our car is damaged by a hit-and-run driver. We lose our wallet or keys, or our purse is stolen. Our luggage is lost, or our flight is delayed or cancelled. We are diagnosed with cancer. Our parents become ill, or their behavior radically changes. Someone is rude to us.

No amount of anger, yelling, worry, or desire for revenge changes what is real in the moment at hand. Only by accepting the present circumstance for what it is, rather than what we think it should, would, or could be, can we help ease the stress and upset that come from the misconception that we can control or change people and the uncontrollable situations of life.

MEDITATIONS AND EXERCISES

Here is an exercise that will help you practice acceptance:

The next time something happens in life that upsets your plans, take a deep breath. Slow down. Count to five.

Relax into the truth that only by accepting what is real in the present can you take the necessary action to leave an abusive relationship. Or rebound from losing a job. Or seek help for an addiction. Or deal with an illness. Or appropriately honor the memory of a loved one.

Sit down in a quiet place and write down your answers to these questions:

1. What areas in your life would improve by your patient acceptance of what is?

2. It's common to want to control how others respond to you. When have you attempted this? How did it turn out? What were you able to control, and what weren't you able to control? How can you apply this insight to your other relationships?

3. Do you remember a time when you ignored the truth of another person's behavior in favor of what you wanted him or her to be? What steps can you take to be more accepting of others, warts and all?

4. Have you ever ignored the truth of your own behavior in favor of a fantasy of who you want to be? What steps can you take to be more accepting of yourself, warts and all?

Set Boundaries

For more than five years, I turned the other cheek and stayed publicly silent about the angry behavior of a friend. Meanwhile, she sent repeated e-mails, letters, and phone calls promising to seek help to ease the torment that caused her to treat her loved ones badly. Though my friend was quick to share her intentions of change, she continued to spew anger. Over time I grew weary of forcing myself to endure the inevitable degradation of our get-togethers because of her rage, and one day I told her I was done.

While I was caring for my father after he experienced life-threatening complications from surgery, I took a phone call from a close family member who refused to stop criticizing my father's health-care professionals. After several minutes of listening to his familiar negativity, I spoke up. I told him that going back in time to recreate what he thought should have happened was not only impossible, but it did nothing to support me, my father, or the current situation. He hung up on me.

These were not the first, second, third, or fourth instances of unacceptable behavior that were forced on me by two people who said they loved me. It was not the fifth, sixth, or seventh time I had asked them to stop. For years I consistently reached out to both my friend and my family member, forgave, and moved on. No matter how my heart ached for them to behave differently, the time came when I needed to respect myself and set boundaries.

There is a perception that those who live a heart-centered life are submissive and must turn the other cheek, regardless of how we are treated. While tolerance, patience, cooperation, forgiveness, and peacefulness are behaviors of living aligned with heart, so is setting boundaries. To civilly but firmly set boundaries is one way we care for and respect ourselves. Healthy boundaries are a necessary part of creating wholesome relationships with others.

The truth is, you and I can only be half of any relationship, and our goal is to be the best half we can be. Whether we are interacting with our partner, family, friends, co-workers, the checker at the market, or a stranger we meet on the street, we are only able to be our best half by treating others with respect. We remain patient and try to set a peaceful and harmonious example. Those who say they love us and yet treat us badly, we ask to stop. When our repeated efforts and requests are continuously met with unacceptable behavior, there comes a point when we have to ask ourselves what value or benefit we are receiving from the relationship.

We do not have to walk in someone else's shoes before we choose not to follow in his or her footsteps. No matter how much we desire to support other people or have a good relationship with those we love, it is not always possible. There are those whose pain is so deep they are terrified to look within themselves for the answers necessary to ease their suffering. They become accustomed to lashing out, thoughtlessly inflicting their anger, insecurity, fear, and control issues onto those they say they love. No matter how much we may want to help someone who is hurting, or addicted, or emotionally detached, or abusive, or being abused, that person must want to make the change for him or herself.

When I hurt other people, it was because I was hurting. Without thinking or minding, I irresponsibly took my frustration and disappointment out on others instead of looking within to find the source(s) of my pain. One day I found the courage to honestly look at myself, and I began to uncover and heal my hurt. Dealing with my own wounds helped me rein in my behavior, be mindful, and stop taking my pain out on myself and others.

We cannot control the behavior of or change anyone except ourselves. One of the hard truths about life is that, for our own contentment and peace, we must remember people change for the better only when they really want to.

Once we recognize there is something in us we'd like to change, each of us is capable of amazing personal transformation. But there must be recognition and a burning desire to shift ourselves for the better. Without this, there will be no real effort, no purposeful steps forward.

Regardless of whom our relationship is with, and despite how much we may care for that person, it is healthy to admit there are some people who do not respect or control themselves. Without self-control and self-respect, a person is not capable of being a positive part of a loving and considerate relationship.

Loving another person does not mean we should enable him or her to mistreat us. Loving means not abusing or mistreating anyone for any reason. People who do not treat us with kindness, respect, and courtesy are not expressing love. So, it is necessary that we set boundaries out of love for ourselves. We do so by learning what boundaries are, what they are not, and the steps involved in establishing clear limits.

What Boundaries Are

People will treat us as we allow them to. A boundary is a limit we set to protect and take care of ourselves. Boundaries let other people know our availability, values, and the conditions under which we will interact. Healthy, clearly communicated boundaries identify our needs, feelings, and rights in relationship to others. Boundaries let others know we respect and value ourselves.

It's essential that we establish and maintain limits to protect ourselves and create positive relationships with others. Boundaries help us determine the things we want to do and those we don't and if we're clear on what those boundaries are from the start, they help us to stand up for ourselves without guilt for putting our needs first.

Without establishing (and articulating) the behaviors we will and will not tolerate from others, we leave ourselves open to becoming angry and resentful about how we are allowing ourselves to be treated. That leads us to taking our pain out on others and ourselves. So, healthy, clearly communicated boundaries let others see we respect and value ourselves. And, respecting the needs, feelings, and boundaries of others lets them see they are valued.

What Boundaries Are Not

Establishing how we want to be treated is not about control or manipulation. We do not set boundaries to change other people. We do so to change us—to create a better, more positive life for ourselves by demonstrating a commitment to self-love and respect.

Boundaries clearly state what behavior is hurtful to us, yet we do not have expectations of any particular outcome. That is, we set boundaries for ourselves while realizing the other person is completely responsible for making changes to his or her behavior.

How to Set Boundaries

Through counseling and a lifetime of trial and error, I learned that setting strong, lasting boundaries with ourselves and others requires us to do four things:

- Define acceptable behavior;
- Accept that doing nothing is condoning bad treatment;
- Express our feelings calmly and clearly; and
- Be comfortable with not being popular.

We'll cover each of these things in detail next, so you can begin to come up with your own plan of action for setting boundaries in your life.

DEFINE ACCEPTABLE BEHAVIOR

Have you heard the song "You Always Hurt the One You Love"? The truth is that love does not hurt. Love does not abuse. Love does not take advantage. Love is not impatient. Love is not critical. Love is not controlling. Love is not angry.

We learn how to behave from our family, friends, peers, and television. But that does not mean the behavior we were taught or exposed to is acceptable. Hitting, screaming, inappropriate touching, humiliation, rage, control, dishonesty, recklessness, blame, jealousy, lying, cheating, stealing, sexual abuse, physical and psychological abuse, projection, denial, etc., are mistreatment, and they are not the loving behaviors that create a positive life. Negative behavior hurts.

For so much of my life, I was very confused when people told me, "I love you." Because I grew up with mistreatment that was often considered acceptable behavior, I did not know how to set boundaries with the people in my life. Even if I tried to take a stand and say no, I was often ignored, my feelings and wants simply discounted.

As a result, I endured abusive behavior. Rather than speak up, I felt safer blending in, becoming invisible. When conflicts arose, I didn't want to make waves. I wanted to keep peace and be the one who smoothed over unpleasant situations. Even when I was threatened with physical harm by a babysitter who was molesting me, I did not speak up.

I made it into adulthood with still virtually no boundaries. For many years, I continued to let the opinions and behaviors of others overrule what I knew was best for me. Every time I did what other people wanted, or behaved in ways that went against my values in order to fit in with the crowd, or endured and ignored abusive treatment, I suffered.

Through counseling I learned that my avoidance of setting and enforcing healthy boundaries was codependent behavior. My low self-esteem caused me to look outside myself to make me feel better. I ignored other people's negative behavior, preferring to create a fantasy of who I thought they could be. Too often I went along with the crowd, even if that meant putting myself in danger. I repressed my own needs to please other people, and that often resulted in my being treated like a doormat. Not standing up for myself showed a lack of self-respect and made me an easy target for abuse.

It took courage, but when I finally stood up for myself and stopped permitting people to treat me badly, or stopped blindly following others and instead took the actions I knew I needed to take, I felt strong and proud of myself. With practice, setting boundaries became easier. Soon I no longer cared about being disowned by others, because I realized disowning me and my values was the ultimate betrayal.

ACCEPT THAT DOING NOTHING IS CONDONING BAD TREATMENT

Many years ago, I dated a thief. This person thought nothing of stealing. It was as if she were owed something and was entitled to do as she pleased without thought to the consequences of her actions. Her behavior went against my deep core values of honesty and personal accountability, but I felt powerless because I thought turning the other cheek was how I loved someone. But it wasn't. I realized that not standing up against this illegal and irresponsible behavior was actually helping to keep the situation alive.

Albert Einstein said, "No problem can be solved from the same level of consciousness that created it." Part of setting boundaries is accepting that doing nothing is enabling people who behave irresponsibly to continue exposing us to the turbulent wake of their negative behavior.

With the realization that I could change my situation by changing myself, I found tremendous power in learning to establish limits with people who disrespected and mistreated me. Often those boundaries required me to leave people who were physically abusive and whose behavior exposed me to danger. It was hard, but no matter how many promises were made or how many times they apologized for their behavior, I finally realized that people who mistreat, abuse, and are dishonest with themselves and others will say anything to keep the situation as it is. People who have grown accustomed to treating themselves and others poorly are not going to change unless they truly want to, and often not unless they get professional help with doing so. Only by leaving relationships did my situation change for the better, regardless of if theirs did or not.

EXPRESS YOUR FEELINGS
CALMLY AND CLEARLY

When you're setting boundaries, it is vital to communicate clearly and without blame (even if the other person is guilty). Remember, these limits are designed for your protection and self-respect. That means staying focused on directly communicating about someone's behavior, how it makes you feel, and how you desire to be treated differently.

Here are a few examples of how you can share your boundaries with others in a clear, respectful way:

"When you steal, I feel betrayed, fearful, and responsible. Please do not take things that do not belong to you."

"I feel sad, blamed, and attacked when you speak to me disrespectfully. Please treat me with patience and respect."

"Please pick up after yourself. When you leave your dirty clothes on the floor expecting me to pick them up, I feel disgusted and used."

"I feel betrayed and abandoned when you charge purchases to the credit cards after we've agreed not to. Please honor the agreements we make."

When we identify hurtful behavior, the goal is to communicate our feelings and desires peacefully, directly, and specificallly. If we are met with resistance, we should try to tell the person the consequences of ignoring our request. This doesn't need to be a threat—but oftentimes having someone tell us the consequences of our actions lets us know how important the issue is. In the case of violence, contact the authorities.

Unless you are in immediate physical danger, or the situation has escalated to the point that you and the other person have stopped listening to one another, you can establish a boundary in the moment. If there is clear communication, you do not have to wait to express your needs; you can make an immediate request that he or she stop the behavior. A cooling off period is usually necessary for everyone involved to be in a different, more receptive space.

Regardless of if your boundary is set over something as seemingly small as your tolerance for dirty laundry or as crucial as protecting yourself from physical harm, you must be willing to do whatever it takes to remain true to yourself. That means not picking up dirty laundry after you've said you can't do it anymore. It means not tolerating your chronically late friend being late again, just one more time. Do not pay your drug-addicted child's rent or car payment after you've said enough. Because every time you relent, you validate and condone that unacceptable behavior and enable others to continue behaving badly at your expense.

BE COMFORTABLE
WITH NOT BEING POPULAR

Setting a boundary is one thing, but unless we are willing to enforce it, no matter how small or large, the people (children too) with whom we have set the boundary will not take us seriously. Consistency is a critical part of maintaining our self-respect. And remaining true to our boundaries is especially important, because establishling limits is not always popular.

I have set countless boundaries with people over the course of my life, and I was not popular for doing so. When I decided I was worth more than how I was being treated, it was like shining a spotlight on other people's behavior. But I learned to remain strong, to do what I knew in my heart was the more enlightened and peaceful action. Now, if the situation remains unchanged, I do not waver.

One holiday I was "obligated" by the unwritten rules of society and family to attend an event that I said I would not attend again. I did not confirm I would go. It was assumed.

Over the years, I had endured repeated misdirected and irresponsible anger at similar family gatherings. Each one turned into a shouting match, or a denigrating discussion of politics, or an argument over a movie. After a history of consistently negative events, I had had enough. I set a boundary out of love for myself by communicating what behavior was unacceptable and why.

While I accept that people change, and I have forgiven each of the parties involved in the previous unpleasant family gatherings, forgiveness does not mean I have forgotten the pain. Although it was expected that I would attend this gathering, I chose not to. So I completely understand how hard it is to set and uphold boundaries with those we care for who do not recognize how to behave in loving and respectful ways.

Just because setting a boundary with people becomes uncomfortable for them does not mean we must back down. We do not have to be unkind, but we do have to remain strong. Remember that saying no and setting a boundary with abusive, irresponsible, or controlling people is challenging their behavior or the hold they think they have on us. But we are completely in charge of our own power. We do not give our power away by feeling guilty or allowing others to talk us out of the decisions we've made for our greater good. Remember, refusing to go back on a boundary we have set is bringing a greater level of positive awareness to a negative situation.

Part of treating ourselves respectfully is to bravely and firmly stay the course, no matter what anyone else says or how many attempts are made to manipulate us into changing our mind. Think about this: If someone is able to justify mistreating others, they are being dishonest with themselves. So how can we expect they will be honest with us? Regardless of why a boundary is necessary, we are responsible for setting and upholding it. While we hope for the best, we are not responsible if the other person chooses to defy or ignore the boundary.

Have you heard the saying "Misery loves company"? Well, it is true. There was a time in my life when I was miserable and wanted other people around who validated my suffering and supported me in feeling bad. Yet, when I honestly looked at my relationships, I realized I detested being around miserable people.

To heal, be content, and have a peaceful life, I needed to surround myself with people who were creating joyful, balanced, and peaceful lives. Wow! What a difference that made.

Negative, abusive, or controlling relationships neither contribute to our joy nor assist us in having our best life. There is no rule that says we have to accept continuously negative behavior from anybody, especially not from those who say they love us.

While we cannot hope to control or change other people, we do have the power to cut off associations with people who bring us down, are consistently negative, expose us to dangerous circumstances, or tell us who we should be rather than supporting the best of who we are. Creating the best life requires learning to set beneficial boundaries out of love for ourselves—both with other people and with ourselves.

Set Boundaries with Yourself

Other people did not take the actions necessary for me to quit smoking or lose over fifty pounds. Other people did not earn my master's degree for me, heal my painful past, or teach me to forgive and love myself.

On my journey of healing, I got other people's advice. I went to a counselor. I attended support groups. Yet no matter who or what I brought in to help, no matter how good the guidance, I did not achieve the healing I wanted until I realized I am the only one capable of taking action. So I took charge of changing my behavior, ending my fears, and quieting my hypercritical and egotistical mind. By becoming accountable for me, I learned to respect and trust myself, which led to self-love. Self-love allowed me to become a thoughtful, restrained, and caring person with others.

To better my life, I had to better myself by defining what I considered to be acceptable behavior. Then I set boundaries in order to achieve those goals. And there were many times I was not popular with myself for striving to change for the better.

While I was getting over the withdrawals of smoking, there were countless times I wanted just one more cigarette. But the boundary I had set was not to pick up even one cigarette ever again. To be stronger than the addiction, temptation, and my countless rationalizations, I had to focus with tunnel vision on keeping the boundary firmly in place. Concentrating on the boundary I set with myself gave me the willpower to stop smoking cold turkey. It has been many years since I put cigarettes down, and the boundary of not having even one cigarette remains in place.

Setting Healthy Boundaries Takes Time

Changing behaviors, such as learning to communicate feelings clearly or asking for what we want, takes time. During the learning process, be patient with yourself and others and allow time for change. If sufficient time has passed without positive movement, try setting the boundary again or refuse to participate. Remember, one of the most courageous acts of self-love is to stop "should" relationships. Just because someone is family or a longtime friend does not mean you must continue to have them in your life or "should" allow them to continue behaving badly. Instead, surround yourself with responsible and respectful people. People who are creating their lives with positive purpose are everywhere, and they are eager to support your journey of leading with your heart.

MEDITATIONS AND EXERCISES

Sit down in a quiet place and write down your answers to these questions:

1. Are there people in your life who say they love you but who hurt you just the same? Who are they, and how have they hurt you?

2. Have you ever hurt the ones you love?

3. What boundaries can you set with others out of love for yourself? How will setting these limits improve your life?

4. What steps can you take to set boundaries and communicate them to others? Ask someone you trust for support.

5. What boundaries do you want to set with yourself? How will setting self-limits improve your life? What practical steps can you take right now to begin to set these boundaries? Make a list beginning with the easiest step to the hardest and keep it in a safe place where you can refer to it. Try to accomplish one thing and then cross it off. How does it feel? Then try the next step on your list. Ask someone you trust for support.

Note: If you or someone you know is suffering emotional abuse, seek a counselor or support group, or call your local helpline. If you are experiencing physical abuse, immediately tell a trusted friend and contact the police.

NOTES

Trust Your Inner Knowing

When I was five years old, my mom and dad took me horseback riding. The horse was large, and she had recently given birth. My parents barely got me in the saddle when suddenly the mare took off. She ran as fast as possible down a dirt road, leaving my stunned parents in the dust.

Never having ridden a horse before, I had no idea what to do. I clung to the saddle horn for dear life. As the horse feverishly galloped down the road, I became aware of a silent, yet comforting, "knowing" within that offered, *Lean down and hold the neck.* Without hesitation I followed its direction.

The horse continued to race down the road, then abruptly turned and headed to a nearby shed. She ducked to avoid the low-hanging tin roof. Because I was holding on and leaning beside her neck, I avoided injury—maybe even death.

In high school, I was not part of the in crowd. Once I was asked out on a double date by a young man who was very popular. You may remember certain kids who walked the halls and caused wakes of envy as they passed. If you do, you might appreciate my adolescent excitement at being included in a world I did not dream possible. Yet there is often a huge disparity between the way we fantasize someone to be and how they really are.

The young man drove like a maniac all over town, speeding through neighborhoods at seventy miles an hour. He endangered himself and his passengers as he moved ever closer to the edge of losing control. From beginning to end, I was terrified.

Even through my fear, I became aware of a quiet yet firm presence within that advised, *Go home now!* The advice felt so calming and empowering that I asked right away to be taken home. Without caring what anybody thought, I no longer wanted to hang out with him. I began to question why he was part of the in crowd and why he was deemed someone to be admired and emulated.

About a month later, his reckless driving was determined to be the cause of a severe automobile accident. Although injured quite badly, the young man lived. His sister did not.

When I was in my mid-thirties, I was driving home during a strong thunderstorm. The rain was coming in torrents. The wind was blowing so hard I could not see. Out of the blue, I became aware of a forceful internal message urging me, *Stop NOW!* I did. A split second later, a huge oak tree crashed in front of my truck, landing right in front of my bumper.

You and I are home to an unexplainable intuitive guidance. The counsel we receive from this wise and loving presence is often protective, as the previous examples demonstrated. Sometimes a mysterious awareness arrives to help us avoid doing something we feel is not in our best interest, such as cosigning a loan for an irresponsible relative (or anyone, for that matter). Perhaps the message is to pass on an invitation to go out with someone who is handsome and entirely self-absorbed. Maybe we need to turn down a job offer even though we need the work because something does not feel right about the situation. Possibly it is our intuition that prompts us to go back to the grocery store counter where we absentmindedly left our car keys.

Each of us has access to this aware, watchful guidance inside us. To benefit from its direction, we learn to trust that our inner intuitive wisdom is more accurate than the information offered by our often biased and self-centered minds.

No one ever advised me, "Regina, trust your gut." I was not taught that my conscious inner wisdom, hunch, or comprehension was more accurate than my mind. My formal and religious education did not address listening to and acting on perceptive directives from my heart. Our current society still places its highest value on intellectual prowess and mental function.

Parents wait in line to enroll their very young children in programs to prepare them for kindergarten. Our educational institutions teach us to examine the external world. These programs are primarily intended to challenge us to judge what we see, to think critically, and to appraise what goes on outside of us. Yet the guidance you and I receive from the higher, wiser part of our being is distinct from our rational and logical thoughts developed in formal education. A lifetime of experience taught me the key to benefiting from our internal knowing is to learn to trust its wisdom over our thoughts.

When I was downsized from an executive position, I did not appreciate how tight the job market was. After several months of searching unsuccessfully for work in my preferred field, I opened myself to a wider range of possibilities.

I interviewed with a physician for a job in a busy practice in a small Texas town, and it went well. The physician was pleasant, and the position seemed to be a good match for what I was seeking. Unfortunatelly, I did not have the same experience in a follow-up interview with the physician's partner, and I'd be working with both physicians closely.

Although she was congenial, I had a nagging hunch that all was not as it seemed. I was not able to put my finger on exactly what it was, I just knew something was not right. When I was offered the position, even though I needed the work, I turned it down. Only a few weeks later, I learned the physicians had dissolved the partnership, the practice suffered, and widespread staff layoffs resulted.

You and I receive these kinds of messages each day, but we often do not act on our higher inner awareness. One reason is that we have a tendency to embark on a fantastical mind voyage of creating what we want to be true, rather than using our intuition to help us determine what is really true.

My thoughts attempted to convince me I was making up the tension between the physicians. My thoughts went on to justify how, if the tension was not imaginary, my accepting the job would help the situation.

Our rational mind—and its thoughts—will defend what it offers as more appropriate and intelligent than the wisdom of our quiet inner voice. We must be wary any time we feel stress, fear, or confusion in our gut, or when our thoughts create a rationalization about someone or a situation. These feelings are a clear indication our mind is judging people and situations based on what it *wants* to be true. When we pay attention to advice such as *Slow down,* or *Wait, where are my keys?* or *Stop NOW!* we can take the recommended action.

When other people are involved, we take time to ask ourselves questions such as, "What makes me think my irresponsible relative will be responsible this time?" Or "What is it about this handsome stranger that feels off?" Taking time to genuinely care about the answers causes us to place great value on the input from our higher, internal guidance.

To avoid problems and have the best, safest, most trouble-free life possible, it pays to trust our inner knowing. Without fail, each time we courageously act upon its protective, loving, and responsible guidance, life is better for it.

MEDITATIONS AND EXERCISES

Sit down in a quiet place and write down your answers to these questions:

1. When have you discounted your inner wisdom, only to later learn that it was indeed correct? What do you

think would have happened had you followed your heart in that situation?

2. When did you act upon your inner guidance? What was the outcome?

Here are a few exercises that will help you connect to your inner knowing:

1. Find a serene space, such as under a tree. Sit and observe the world around you. Keep your mind quiet. Note the colors and textures of the flowers and trees and clouds. Listen to the sound of birds and the leaves rustling in the breeze. Focus on your senses to go beyond your mind and into your inner self.

2. Create a place of reverence in your home. Make it a space where you can light a candle or incense. Put out items that lift you up—photos of special people who inspire you, fresh flowers, or other treasures and keepsakes. Close your eyes and pay attention to your breathing. Slow down. Sit for five or ten minutes and ask Spirit to awaken your awareness to your deeper knowing.

3. When you eat, slow down to really taste and smell the food. Envision it nurturing your body. When you shower, feel the water on your body. Smell the soap. Stay aware of what you are doing, but at the same time try to clear your mind of specific thoughts. Quiet your mind and allow yourself to be fully present with each action. When you are present with a still mind you can hear your inner self.

NOTES

Define Success for Yourself

I no longer own a car or drive with any regularity, and I have never felt more free.

Over my lifetime I have owned three homes. Today, I live in a one-bedroom apartment and have never felt more at home.

I do not have the latest mobile technology, and I have never felt more connected.

I may seem a failure to those whose main focus is cars, homes, and gadgets, yet I have never felt more successful. I wake each day contented, peaceful, and fulfilled, and more in love with life. No thing has ever offered me this.

It took many years to identify what success means to me. Each time I look at my dogs, I am reminded of what a joy it is to responsibly provide for their well-being. Today, people tell me they want to come back as one of my pets. When I think of purchasing a car, fuel efficiency and environmental and financial responsibility top my list of must-haves. Instead of surrounding myself with many items, I save up and purchase fewer things of better quality. Years ago, I learned that no matter what the item is, whether toilet paper, toys, or appliances, cheap is actually quite expensive, since something of inferior quality neither lasts as long nor is as reliable, and so much waste negatively impacts the environment.

I am no longer impressed with people who set my worth by what I wear, what I own, where I live, and what I drive. After successfully climbing out of the turbulent waters of debt, living within my means has become an important standard I've set for myself.

While I do not have the car or home or popular technology, I am free of debt. Each day I enjoy friends, family, strangers, and the breathtaking beauty that surrounds me. I am free of the burden of too much stuff. Every day I work on doing my part to make the world a better, more peaceful, cleaner, more cooperative place. I am connected to my heart, to other people, to the natural world, and to our planet. I am in command of and responsible for my thoughts and behavior. I am at home in my charming apartment as well as in my heart. Now these are my benchmarks for success.

There is nothing wrong with having wealth, positions, and honors. I believe what we want to receive from life and what we want to leave as our legacy are important questions to ask. Regardless of what other people use as their benchmarks, we have to define success for ourselves. If the only thing we achieve in life is a reputation for being compassionate, honest, and responsible, that is legacy enough.

MEDITATIONS AND EXERCISES

Sit down in a quiet place and write down your answers to these questions:

1. Do you live within your means?
2. Do you have six to eight months of savings to cover expenses if you get laid off or experience an extended illness?
3. What does success mean to you? Money? Health? Romance? Happiness?
4. In what ways do you feel successful?
5. What steps can you take to further your feelings of success?

Tip: Your joy and peace with life come from choosing quality over quantity. Less really is more.

Here is an exercise that will help you define success for yourself:

Have you noticed how we can easily be influenced by peer pressure? Generally we think this applies to children or young adults, who often blindly follow the crowd and leap before they look. However, adults are perhaps just as easily influenced by what other people think and do.

I believe one of the most important actions we take is to think for ourselves and not simply follow the lead (beliefs, opinions, rationalizations, gossip, etc.) of other people. To look before we leap is really good advice, and doing so is living responsibly.

NOTES

You Create What You Want in Life

I took a course for my master's program in management called "Strategic Planning and Implementation" about the process an organization undertakes to outline a course of action designed to achieve its goals. A third of the way through the semester, it hit me. I experienced discontent and dissatisfaction from going through life by the seat of my pants. Without a plan and sincerely evaluating my strengths and weaknesses, I had no clue as to what actions I needed to take to create what I wanted in life.

I was forty-eight years old before I found my right partner. It happened only after I stopped focusing on finding someone and concentrated completely on being someone worth finding. Until that point, I'd never considered the values, spiritual beliefs, and behaviors that were important to me in relationships. And, I did not realize the importance of needing to display these values for myself before I could find someone else with them, too. To have any chance of creating the fulfilling, positive relationship I wanted, I first had to determine who I was, what I wanted in a partner, and how I needed to behave in a relationship.

Who am I? There was a time when I focused on things I thought were wrong with me. One day I got fed up with constantly feeling inadequate. I sat down and made a list of all that is right with me and what I believed was wrong with me. That gave me motivation to either accept the things I thought were wrong, or change them.

I was sick and tired of all of the fear and negativity being shoved at me, so I decided to apply the same idea to life in general. Yes, there is conflict, suffering, and malevolence in the world. But there is also positivity. I made the decision to no longer allow myself to be brought down by the steady stream of what the media or other people wanted me to believe about what was wrong with the world. I began to look for, and keep my attention on, that which was going right and to change the negative things I could.

Seriously thinking about all I was, the positive and negative, allowed me to identify areas that needed change. I was kind, loyal, generous, organized, determined, and hard-working, and I loved animals and the natural world. Then I focused on honestly listing negative beliefs or behaviors that limited me.

Being insecure, closed, cautious, and emotionally unavailable permeated my relationships. My low self-esteem disconnected me from my feelings and did not allow me to communicate clearly. Codependent, I sought validation from the outside world. Unresolved issues of abandonment and unworthiness made me fear being alone. Setting healthy boundaries out of love and respect for myself was not part of my skill set.

I rushed from relationship to relationship, yet, once in, I became distant, not wanting to be hurt or used. While projecting my pain, negative thoughts, anger, and suspicions onto others, I also looked to other people to rescue me from a confusing and painful past.

The negative list was revealing, but instead of feeling saddened by the process of candidly identifying my limiting beliefs and behaviors, I felt empowered. Having the courage to look at myself honestly generated a crucial to-do list.

After completing a personal inventory, I made a list of what I wanted in a relationship. Then I had to make certain the values and beliefs I identified were a genuine part of me. I wanted clear, open, and honest communication, so I focused on learning to be a good communicator. Since I desired someone who had either worked through or was actively addressing their limiting personal issues, I became devoted to healing my emotional wounds.

Desiring trust, forgiveness, and support, I became trustworthy, forgiving, and supportive. Wanting a responsible and dependable partner, I became accountable and reliable. I concentrated on growing my individuality and spirituality so I would be in the position to encourage and support the same in someone else. I wanted a respectful relationship, so I agreed to treat myself and other people with reverence.

Desiring kindness, honesty, and openness, I focused on being caring, truthful, and friendly. I wanted calm and became dedicated to maintaining a peaceful way of life. Enjoying play, I wanted someone who also consciously made time for fun. Because I desired encouragement, I learned to support others. Desiring intimacy, I became emotionally available, to myself and to other people. Longing to share my dreams, concerns, and wants, I readily became a person who holds the aspirations, apprehension, and desires of others safely within my heart.

When I took time to identify what makes up a good partnership, I also realized the important role compatibility plays in finding a suitable companion. Knowing I wanted to be in a monogamous relationship allowed me to exclude those who practice infidelity. My love of animals caused me to question the reality of having a good relationship with someone who disliked my furry friends. Valuing promptness and neatness, I stopped myself from getting involved with someone who was continuously late or who did not value personal hygiene and tidiness. Placing great importance on spirituality, I desired someone who would support, encourage, and be patient with my heart-growth.

One of our principal reasons for being alive is to learn to live with principles. Through the personal planning process, I realized that to have the best life we need to bring the best of ourselves to life. To be our best, it is necessary to assess our strengths and weaknesses. Below is a pyramid of positive personal values

Wise

HUMBLE

Happy Calm

Lighthearted OPEN Joyful

Neat Fun FAIR JUST Safe AWARE

Willing Listener *Joyful* SECURE *Flexible*

Present *Skillful* Loving STABLE PLAYFUL Serene

POSITIVE PERSONAL VALUES

Decisive *Curious* Healthy *Friendly* STRONG Orderly

Creative Talented Value Life ACCURATE Tolerant

Punctual Visionary Ambitious Powerful Practical *Tranquil*

Conscious ORGANIZED *Delightful* Persistent *Successful* Generous Spiritual

Productive Purposeful DISCIPLINED Honorable Observant HUMOROUS INNOVATIVE

HARD WORKING LAW ABIDING Communicator Progressive Adventurous

Courageous CHANGEABLE Resourceful Impeccable Competent Responsive Independent leader *Graceful*

Good Person Accountable Harmonious *Time Manager* WHOLESOME Reverent IMAGINATIVE

Self-Improving *SELF-ASSESSING* Problem Solver Self-Respect SELF-ESTEEM *Accomplished*

Environmental Advocate Detail Oriented Collaborative knowledgeable ENTHUSIASTIC Balanced

that are strong points when they are a part of our behavior and limitations when they are not. What we value motivates our actions.

Positive values provide the self-awareness, wisdom, and self-control that equip us to weigh the consequences of our actions before we act. Values give us the courage to act upon what we respect and to remain true to ourselves regardless of what anyone else does or believes. Adhering to what we value keeps us steadfast on the cliff above when those around us obey their mind's rationalizations and dive into the murky water below. When behavior is based on positive values, it gifts us with the power to control our actions and to create life from our responsible heart. When we know what we value, we will know what values to look for in a partner and friends. And we will know what values to teach our children so they too can create lives of love, compassion, and purpose.

Take time to determine which values are currently among your advantages, or, if absent, your disadvantages. This is an opportunity to be completely honest and open with yourself. Consult a dictionary if you're questioning the meaning of certain words. You may also want to highlight or circle your current values so you can clearly see areas needing work.

After determining your values, strengths, and limitations, spend time determining your objectives. Sit down with pen and paper and outline a plan of action to realize your goals. Then believe in yourself. Remain committed. Take the actions necessary to be successful.

Do you realize why superheroes are called action heroes? Because there is no such thing as a hope hero!

Each success we achieve in life is the result of our being emotionally invested in the outcome, to the point that we make ourselves take the consistent actions necessary to create what we want. For twenty-two years I wanted to quit smoking. My plans were good. Yet hoping to accomplish something did not actually make it happen. After passing up a cigarette or two, soon I'd make an excuse to have just one. Then I would beat myself up for once again not being strong enough not to smoke. Excusing my lack of commitment, I would tell myself I was not perfect, I was only human, with faults, and allowed to make mistakes.

I attempted to change my negative habits for a long, long time, until I realized I could continue "trying" for the rest of my life. Quitting smoking—or any other destructive habit—is accomplished not by trying harder, but by *doing*. I actually had to make myself *not* pick up a cigarette until I no longer had the desire to smoke, which took about a month. To stop smoking cold turkey I relied on my personal values of being aware, strong, and accountable. These and other positive values fueled my willpower to not smoke even one cigarette.

Yes, intending to accomplish something is a great first step. Aiming to improve ourselves starts us thinking about the personal changes we want to make or evaluating what career, educational, relationship, and financial goals to set. Yet the statements "I hope to lose weight," "I aim to be financially independent," "I propose to be patient in traffic jams," "I plan to be peaceful," and "I mean to be successful" still point to some change to happen at a future time.

"Plan," "hope," or "I am trying" gives us permission to wait another day. And when given the option, all too often we will not begin any action at all. We will lie awake at night fretting, disappointed and frustrated by our lack of progress, but we will not act.

But a small shift in perspective can make all the difference. By changing the planning statement of "I want" to the present-moment statement of "I am," we can remain mindful of the negative habit. It also helps us stay emotionally connected to the behavior. For example, "I am losing weight" supports us in being more mindful about eating with awareness and passing up the elevator in favor of the stairs. "I am saving money" prompts us to stop before purchasing yet another pair of jeans in favor of achieving the goal of having money left over at the end of each month. "I am a nonsmoker" really does help consciously break the habit by allowing us to visualize ourselves without cigarettes. I could go on, but I think you get the idea. "I am" is a simple yet powerful positive affirmation that actually motivates us to take the daily steps necessary to accomplish our goals.

To change ourselves or a relationship, we must be willing to do whatever it takes to accomplish the goal. Change won't happen just by investing a few hours in a workshop, a religious service, or a counseling session. Creating new, positive habits is an entire lifestyle change, and it takes time to replace old habits with new ones. Living changed becomes our reason for being, our moment-by-moment priority.

When stumbling blocks come up, and they will for all of us, do not take no for an answer. Rely on your values to support you in taking the necessary actions over and over until your new, positive lifestyle is securely in place.

You are absolutely capable of making the personal changes you want to make once you stop "trying" and instead do, do, do. Determine your strengths and weaknesses. Choose something you want to change in your life. Make a list of the steps necessary to accomplish and maintain your goal. Then become an action hero. Put your heart into it and claim "I am" as your present-moment statement of purpose. Use this to move yourself from point A, the desire of what you want, to point B, creating what you want.

Once you've defined the life you want, the following chapters will help you to create it.

MEDITATIONS AND EXERCISES

Here is an exercise that will help you create the life you want:

To have the best life, focus on the positive. Sit down and make two lists. On the right, list those things "right" with you. On the left, list the things you want to change. At this point, you have a choice: you can either accept the things you think are wrong (they aren't that bad), or you can change them. How do you plan to change these weaknesses into strengths? What do you want to accomplish within the next week? In the next month? How about the next year? Five years? Keep your answers in your purse or wallet and refer to them regularly.

Now do the same thing with life in general. Look for and focus on what is positive around you. Being positive does not mean being blind to the negativity in the world. Staying positive is like choosing the role of lighthouse. We purposely illuminate our piece of the world so others can see that regardless of what we face, staying positive is the way to create the happiest, most peaceful and fulfilling life.

Practice Every Day

For years I played fast-pitch softball. Through practice I determined beforehand what I would do in a given situation. I learned to anticipate the best action to take when the ball was hit to me or a teammate. The situation was constantly changing with the placement of the runners on base and the number of outs, so I needed to decide before the ball was hit what I would do. Although it was not possible to make every decision perfectly beforehand, practicing different scenarios dramatically increased the percentage of time I got a play right. And I still made mistakes.

The goal of practice is not to be perfect. Perfection does not exist. Major League Baseball Gold Glove winners are a good example of people who consistently do their best to be the best. These elite players rarely walk away with the coveted award for having performed flawlessly. Any player bestowed a Gold Glove has earned the honor by doing his very best, in each and every activity, more often than not. Leading with your heart is about doing your best to be your best, because creating your best thoughts and behavior takes practice.

The people and circumstances in your life are continually shifting, offering never-ending challenges and opportunities for positive change. That means questioning the path you are on and learning to think differently is ongoing; it's a process that becomes second nature with practice.

Practicing continuous self-evaluation may seem daunting if you allow your thoughts to say you are too busy to pay attention to each and every thing you do. You also have the option to tell your mind to slow down, to be one with life and what is going on in the moment. Regardless of how mundane you view an activity, it is within the everyday tasks you perform and interactions you have where the intentional life you want must be created, action by action, because the peace and contentment you desire come from allowing your heart to be the positive motivating force that defines each part of you—mind, body, and spirit.

Mind

A man waiting to make a right turn into a small grocery store parking lot noticed that only two spaces remained. He saw a woman waiting to turn left into the same lot. Knowing it could be some time before oncoming cars would allow her to turn, when the light changed he purposefully held back traffic and motioned that she should enter the lot ahead of him. She did.

The woman was first to arrive at the two adjoining spaces. Instead of pulling into one space she intentionally parked in the middle of both. Shocked, the man stopped his car and got out.

"Excuse me, ma'am. Will you please move your car so I can park too?"

"No, someone will scratch it."

"But I let you turn ahead of me and there are no more parking places. You've taken the last two."

"So what? It is my right."

The man found another parking place and followed the woman into the store. He was furious and shouted at her. She completely ignored him and went about her business.

Each day you have opportunities to practice remaining aligned with your heart's loving, compassionate, and purposeful values or to stoop to the standards other people set for themselves. To consistently have the best life requires acting aligned with your heart. This requires accepting that your mind is not the smartest part of you, no matter how much it tells you it is. The rationalizations and justifications your mind will create to defend ego-boxing behavior cause stress, frustration, and disappointment that can get you into trouble.

To avoid problems and the anxiety that comes from acting impulsively based on your ego means mastering a mind that has a mind of its own. It means learning to think about what you are thinking and questioning the motivations behind the thoughts. You teach yourself to remain present to pay attention to what is most important in the moment. You work to communicate with care to avoid confrontations and misunderstandings. And when you do encounter the hurtful, rude behavior of others, you appreciate the advantages of forgiving so you can move on.

Master a Mind That Has a Mind of Its Own

You are really getting fat, I thought.

No, I am not, I reacted.

Yes, you are! You have gained over fifty pounds. How does hauling around that much extra weight not make you fat? Now you are not only fat, you are a liar too for denying you are fat. Being fat also makes you lazy. How does it feel to be a big, fat, lazy liar?

For many years, my life was created by an arrogant, self-centered mind "committee" of which I was an absentee member. I did not realize the agenda was a steady stream of negativity and fear. From morning until night, the committee deliberated about what I did wrong today, yesterday, or a year ago. It made detailed lists of the unkind things people said or did to me. It focused on the negativity in the world and rationalized receiving what it wanted when it wanted it.

That was a fabulous chair you saw today, I thought.

Yes, it was attractive, I agreed.

It would look wonderful next to the fireplace. Hey, why not buy two?—one for either side, I urged.

I cannot afford one, much less two, I replied, meaning to stay responsible.

Sure you can. Charge them. Pay over time. What is the big deal? You deserve them. Your friends will be impressed, I rationalized.

Before I taught myself to pay attention to and evaluate my thoughts, I did not realize my mind committee would continue to direct, abuse, and confuse me for as long as I allowed it to. When I was overweight, the committee told me. So I ate healthfully and exercised to lose weight. Then it told me I was not doing enough, or it was fine to cheat. Or if I actually lost weight, I would not keep it off.

When I encountered rudeness from other people, I justified my being impolite in turn as defending myself. Yet when I was bad-mannered, the committee chastised me for behaving disrespectfully. If I arrived late to an engagement, my mind rushed to excuse my rudeness by assuring me other people could wait. Getting somewhere early and waiting for others was another story. The committee silently reprimanded those who arrived late.

The constant negative and reprimanding conversations in my mind were crazymaking, preventing me from going to sleep easily and waking me up at night. When I was awake, they would keep me distracted by making up things about me and other people that were not true. I jumped to conclusions without taking the time to determine the truth. I blindly accepted the committee's rationalizations of my irresponsible actions.

Slowing down to stay connected to my own thinking, I began to notice the negativity of my thoughts. My thoughts attempted to convince me other people had it out for me: *The world is filled with bad people. There is reason to live in fear. The things I accumulate define my success.*

My great aha moment came with the realization that each of these thoughts was a big fat lie. I realized my mind is not the smartest part of me, no matter how much it thinks it is.

Jealous thoughts create jealous behavior. Kind thoughts create kind behavior. Revengeful thoughts create revengeful behavior. Peaceful thoughts create peaceful behavior. Our thoughts create our behavior. Our behavior creates our life. It then makes sense that to create our best life, we must stay connected to what we are thinking, and why, so we can change jealously to kindness, revenge to peace.

The mind does not care if your thoughts are true and rational or not—it just thinks. But with awareness, you can begin to challenge what you are thinking, and see how the mind will create thoughts designed to defend your actions or justify getting what you want. Accepting this truth is vital, because your thoughts create your actions.

My thoughts often condone behaving in ways that result in the exact opposite of what I genuinely want—peace, self-respect, joy, and for life to have real meaning. If I neglected to check posted parking regulations and got a ticket, my initial reaction used to be, *Why me? This is not fair.* Even after I read the sign, my mind still wanted to blame someone else. I would rationalize, *The city only wants my money*, or *I will negotiate with the parking officer.* Somehow I thought I was entitled to be exempt from that rules that applied to everyone else.

Evaluating my thoughts, I realized that placing blame elsewhere for something I did is only self-deceiving. It was not possible to magically go back in time to undo the ticket. I am not entitled to escape the ticket. Making sure to check regulations and not get a ticket again is what I can do.

One time I had a disagreement with a co-worker over a project. Whether by intuitive wisdom or choice, I decided not to become caught up in a discussion with that person and to instead walk away. But as time passed my mind took control and rehashed all the person had ever said or done to me. Two days later, my mind was still focused on those negative thoughts.

In this encounter, being aware and challenging my thoughts

allowed me to return to the present moment. After almost missing an important meeting, I realized my mind was controlling me. Only by becoming aware of these repetitive, nonproductive thoughts was it possible to take control over what I was thinking and retake control of me.

When I was chosen as Peet's customer of the week, my immediate response to having my photo taken was, *You've got to be kidding! On a day I did not wash my hair before coming in. Sure, if you put Angelina Jolie's head on my body.* In a flash, my mind began judging. My mind justified going home, taking a shower, and getting dressed up. It was 6:30 a.m. I had just awakened, and I have never looked like Angelina Jolie. As usual, my mind wanted its way and had the nerve to try and sell me the ridiculous.

Instead of refusing the honor, I quietly told my mind, *Thank you.* I purposefully stopped the unproductive thoughts and followed the barista to the back. I stood against the wall, smiled, and opened my arms wide. The photo was taken. For the next week, all who entered the store saw me as I am early in the morning.

While the mind is not the enemy, it does have its own agenda. My mind is self-absorbed; it does not have my back, nor does it even really care about what is in my best interest. My mind does not stop to hold me accountable. My mind is busy thinking about what it wants to think, whether those thoughts are beneficial or not. My mind wants its way and defends its position, even when presented with evidence to the contrary.

Only by teaching myself to think about what I am thinking, by continuously questioning and evaluating my thoughts, am I able to stop myself from acting upon the often ridiculous thoughts my mind invents. Would buying the chairs really have made me happy? Who wants friends who are more impressed with furniture than they are with my ability to stay financially responsible?

When we slow down to think about what we are thinking while we are thinking it, we learn our mind is a tool. It is great for balancing our checkbook, filling out an income tax report, or working through statistical analysis. It also comes in handy when reading a map, recalling items we need from the grocery store, or learning how to use a remote control. Our mind thinks, and with our heart's wisdom we have the awareness to question those thoughts.

Is what we are thinking real, true, or important? Do our thoughts justify actions that can hurt us or someone else? Are our thoughts attempting to limit the cooperative, inclusive, and virtuous motivations of our heart?

The great seventeenth-century philosopher René Descartes famously said, "I think, therefore I am." While some may view Descartes' statement as equating thinking with being, I believe it is possible his aha moment came as a result of being heart-aware, of thinking about what he was thinking while he was thinking.

Descartes spent much of his life looking for proof of his existence beyond the physical, mental, and emotional aspects and what his five senses provided. Maybe in that moment he got that the higher consciousness of his heart was responsible for monitoring the thoughts within his mind. Being aware of thinking connected him to his conscious self, providing proof of a higher, wiser existence within.

One of the greatest aha moments possible is realizing our mind has a mind of its own. Our mind tells us what we want to hear. Our heart tells us what we need to hear.

Every thought we have, every word we speak, every action we take has the power to hurt or heal. There is a responsible, awake self within our heart, with the power to question our thoughts. Our conscious self is aware of the thoughts we make up about ourselves, situations, and others. Our present self is aware of where our mind wanders. Our higher self has the wisdom to control our impatient, naturally self-absorbed, and often fearful mind. It holds our mind accountable. It encourages us to learn from the choices we make. Our heart strives to improve and desires for us to make a positive contribution.

It was my conscious self that got fed up with the push-me-pull-me craziness of my mind committee's internal deliberations and finally drew a line in the sand. *YOU ARE NOT THE BOSS OF ME!* I screamed silently. *From now on, I am in charge. You will not dictate my actions. You will not tell me what to do. You will not tell me what to think. I am taking my life back!*

Challenging our thoughts is exactly the advice of Marie Pasinski, MD, a Harvard neurologist, brain health expert, and author. No matter how old we are, our brains continue to change, creating new neurons and constructing new neural pathways throughout the course of our life. This process is called neuroplasticity. It is by engaging in new ways of thinking or behaving that these new pathways form. This means we can most certainly fine-tune or even overhaul the voice of our mind committee.

In an article for the *Huffington Post*, Dr. Pasinski suggests:

Improving the tenor of your inner voice begins by listening to what it is saying. When you experience a distressing thought, identify its true nature and give yourself the choice to think or feel differently. In the process, negative thought pathways will wane from disuse and you will begin to forge new self-enhancing neural pathways. When you are feeling joyful and calm, reflect on your accompanying thoughts at that moment. Cherish these thoughts and relish them frequently knowing that these pathways become stronger with each repetition. Over time, you will transform the infrastructure of your brain.

Each moment your mind is flooded with thought. You are constantly processing information. You are not without power over your mind and the thoughts it creates. You are not your thoughts. You are the conscious, present heart-self that is responsible for remaining aware of what you think.

You are the only one who realizes the thoughts you make up. You are capable of stopping your mind from wandering from what you want or need to focus on. You have power to return your thoughts from the past or future to the present. You have control to stop the negative and unproductive conversations of your runaway mind. You have the ability to quiet your mind.

For example, whether you're indoors or outdoors, take a moment to look around. Notice the items that surround you. Let's say you're in your living room, and you notice a throw pillow is out of place. You think to yourself, *That pillow should be over here. How did it get there? I did not move it. Who moved the pillow?*

Your mind's tendency is to attach itself to the pillow or other objects around you. In an instant, you are taken away from looking around to having your mind grab control of your focus. The mind naturally wants to evaluate the pillow, judge its improper placement, and possibly notice a stain on it. This is the mind's constant chatter.

When this happens, you are no longer in charge of what you think about. Your mind has wandered, evaluated, judged, and kept you from viewing the pillow for what it is—just a pillow. The mind does this automatically until you become aware of it. When you notice your mind starting to shift your attention from seeing something as simple as the pillow out of place, reel it back.

Imagine a rod and reel symbolizing awareness over your attention. Become an expert mind-angler. Each time you notice your mind wandering from what you want or need to focus on (like reading this with presence and comprehension), hook your attention and reel your mind back.

Another action that will help you master a mind that has a mind of its own is becoming comfortable with silent stillness. When you keep the television, radio, or stereo on all day and possibly into the night, isn't the goal to keep yourself busy from the time you wake up until you go to sleep? Do you believe the steady stream of activity, noise, and distraction drowns out the constant flow of mind chatter? Do you think you can simply ignore your thoughts and they will go away and stop bugging you? Do you believe the feelings of unworthiness and lack of self-love and respect will magically disappear? In reality, isn't the pain of attempting to drown out your thoughts, instead of dealing with them, overwhelming?

Turn off the music, shut off the television, move away from the computer and cell phone, sit still, and wrap yourself in silence. Now you can actually hear your thoughts and will discover that dealing with the negative mind garbage is not as horrible as you might have feared, or as insurmountable as your mind told you it would be.

Shut off the noise of the world and allow yourself to be comfortable with silent stillness. In silence, you realize you are worthy of self-love and self-respect. In stillness, you learn to hear your quiet inner voice of wisdom. In silence, you become aware of and can change limiting and self-abusive thoughts to those that are limitless and self-supporting. In stillness, you are calm, peaceful, and relaxed. Silent stillness is a cherished friend who nourishes your heart. When all is quiet and still outside you, the quiet and still presence that is you comes forth.

Slow down. Think about what you are thinking. Keep emotionally connected to and responsible for the steady stream of mind chatter. Become aware of how your thoughts subtly limit you. Master a mind that has a mind of its own by learning to identify and change limiting, negative thoughts to positive thoughts that support you in creating the life of meaning you really want.

Do you realize you have power over your thoughts? At one time, being responsible for what I thought and why I was thinking it would have seemed ridiculous. That was before I realized my mind has a mind of its own, and observing these inner thoughts is a crucial part of becoming self-aware.

MEDITATIONS AND EXERCISES

Sit down in a quiet place and write down your answers to these questions:

1. What thoughts cause you fear or worry?
2. What thoughts are limiting you from going for what you want? Are they true, real, productive? Why or why not?
3. What distractions are keeping you from dealing with self-judgment or feelings of unworthiness? How might you get rid of these distractions and gain clarity into what you really want and who you really are?

Here is an exercise that will help you connect with and observe these inner thoughts:

To become familiar with the chatter of your mind committee, sit down in silence and just be an observer as your mind has a conversation with itself. You may use the computer to type the steady stream of thoughts as you are thinking them. Or you may choose to write them down in a journal. The goal is to stay connected to and aware of what you are thinking while you are thinking it. In this way, you learn to continuously evaluate your thoughts so you can change them.

I also encourage you to investigate the benefits of meditation as a daily practice to quiet your mind and connect you to heart.

─────────────────── **NOTES** ───────────────────

Pay Attention to What Is Most Important

When I was sixteen years old, I took a friend for a drive. As I pulled into a driveway to turn around, I looked to my left but not to my right. A car slammed into me as I blindly backed into the street. The other driver was changing the radio station in his car and did not see me. We were both at fault; I was responsible for looking both ways before backing out, and he was responsible for making certain he kept his attention on the road and other drivers.

What if we never accidentally rear-ended the car in front of us? What if we never burned dinner? What if we never interrupted another person? What if we never got a parking ticket, missed a deadline, or had a bank overdraft?

I have yet to meet anybody who is perfect. Going through life without ever making an error is not possible. However, there are countless numbers of people who rise each morning determined to do their best to prevent unnecessary problems.

To lead with our heart, we also strive to consistently do our best. To steadily do our best requires focusing on what is most important in the moment. Keeping ourselves focused on what is important right here, right now, calls for three things.

First, accept we are not more efficient or productive when we attempt to do more than one thing at a time. Second, assume responsibility for purposefully managing the countless distractions and messages we are exposed to each day. Third, deliberately remain present in the now.

STOP MULTITASKING — IT DOESN'T WORK

We live in an attention-deficit world. We navigate within social and business environments that expect us to experience life in nanosecond visual blips and sound bites. To keep up, fit in, or be seen as successful by the world, we buy into the assumption we can and should do more than one thing at once. We believe it saves time. We believe we are being efficient and productive. However, our quality of life resides in remaining present with personal interactions that occur in the moment.

I remember riding in the car with my sister when her children were young. My niece and nephew were in their car seats in the back, and they began hitting each other and crying. My sister calmly moved to the side of the road and stopped the car. Her primary concern as the driver was to ensure our safety. Only after she purposefully kept us safe did she shift her attention to the children.

Each day we hear about accidents that happen as a result of texting, eating, talking on the phone, shaving, or tending to children or pets while driving. With all the things we think we must do in life, it is easy to believe we can and must do several things at once.

Yes, you and I can physically drive and talk on the phone at the same time; but we cannot be fully attentive to either undertaking. Yes, we are able to answer a phone call at work while writing an e-mail, but we cannot do both and remain fully present with either task. Yes, we can sit in on a planning meeting and text at the same time; but it means not being fully conscientious about either activity.

While we may believe we can multitask, it is actually an ego-illusion. As human beings, we cannot pay complete attention to more than one task at a time. Did you know the term "multitasking" actually originated with computers? My computer is able to download photos to a sharing site and run a virus scan while I check e-mail. The computer's processor seems to accomplish multiple tasks at once because of time-sharing. The computer is not actually doing more than a single thing at a time. In reality, it is rotating through several tasks many times a second.

We cannot switch tasks as a computer does. Research shows when we attempt to complete multiple tasks at once, or alternate rapidly between them, the incidence of error goes way up and it takes far longer to accomplish the job than if the tasks were done sequentially.

David E. Meyer, PhD, Director of the Brain, Cognition, and Action Laboratory at the University of Michigan, investigated what happens to us when we attempt to multitask. In a study documented in *Psychological Review*, he found that rather than accomplishing more, we actually slow down significantly.

Dr. Meyer frequently tests Gen M (Generation Multitaskers) students in his lab, and he sees no exception for them, despite their mystique as master multitaskers. Study participants lost huge amounts of time moving between tasks, often adding upwards of 50 percent to completion time.

The toll in terms of slowdown is extremely large—amazingly so. The bottom line is that you can't simultaneously be thinking about your tax return and reading an essay, just as you can't talk to yourself about two things at once. If a teenager is trying to have a conversation on an e-mail chat line while doing algebra, she'll suffer a decrease in efficiency, compared to if she just thought about algebra until she was done. People may think otherwise, but it's a myth. With such complicated tasks [you] will never, ever be able to overcome the inherent limitations in the brain for processing information during multitasking. It just can't be, any more than the best of all humans will ever be able to run a one-minute mile.

The reality of our not being able to successfully divide our attention becomes crystal clear when we try. We have accidents and burn dinner. We leave our cell phone, wallet, or purse on the counter at the bank. We forget our child's piano recital. We do not listen to others carefully, or add instead of subtract an entry in our checkbook. Most importantly, attempting to do many things at once causes us to become emotionally distanced from our heart, other people, and life.

The belief we need to do more than one thing at a time causes us to assume we have the capability to handle everything asked of us, and that this capacity has developed at a rate equal to our intellectual and technological growth. It has not.

MANAGING LIFE'S DISTRACTIONS

While the speed and frequency of information and distractions multiply, our ability to process steadily growing amounts of information and stimuli remains unchanged. Appreciation of our attention as a finite personal resource is not new. Herbert A. Simon, PhD, an influential American social scientist of the twentieth century, noted:

> In an information-rich world, the wealth of information means a dearth of something else; a scarcity of what it is that information consumes. What information consumes is rather obvious: it consumes the attention of its recipients. Hence a wealth of information creates a poverty of attention and a need to allocate that attention efficiently among the overabundance of information sources that might consume it.

We are surrounded, at ever-increasing speed, by amazing innovations that allow interconnectedness on a global scale. Technology creates countless conveniences and wonders. But that does not mean we can interact effectively or establish deep, honest relationships at the same fast pace. With so much demanding our attention, the likelihood is that we will not consider input from our values, experience, and inner knowing. Without these to help guide us, the chance that we will make decisions too rapidly increases.

When we think about it, we realize we are allowing ourselves to be convinced this is how life is supposed to be. It pays to remember that what we concentrate on, we create. And, what we allow in does influence our mental, physical, and emotional well-being.

Do you know Earth is constantly being hit by cosmic radiation? It is.

Do you also know we are constantly being hit, too? We are.

While humans' impact on depleting the ozone layer is cause for worry, exposure to deadly levels of radiation is not going to happen in the immediate future. Of greater concern is that we are being hit, in ways you may not realize, by countless advertisements, news programs, commentary, billboards, radio shows, and websites designed to capture our attention and influence us.

When we pay attention, we realize much of our exposure is negative or opinionated, condones reckless behavior, or promotes the pursuit of meaningless goals. Subtly and overtly, we are struck with untrue messages, such as:

- Sex is love.
- Dyeing our gray hair will automatically attract a much younger love interest.
- Money, fame, the latest technology, and a big home are the keys to fulfillment.
- People who regularly eat fast food look exactly like the models and actors starring in the commercials.
- Opinion is fact.
- What we do on a vacation of limitless temptation has no consequences.
- Life has an "easy" button.
- Beauty is being a size 0.

- Treating other people badly is necessary for success.

- Taking a pill or having elective surgery is the responsible solution for overeating, not exercising, neglecting our body, and depriving ourselves of sleep.

There is a saying, "We are what we eat." What we feed our body can nurture us. Or, eating without awareness can set us up for illness, excess weight gain, and stress. The same is true for what we feed our mind and heart.

We may view the onslaught with the cavalier attitude, "I can just tune it out," or "I am not influenced by it," or "It's just a movie or television show." Yet, scientific research points to how messages and experiences actually change our brain, both positively and negatively.

In *The Brain That Changes Itself*, Canadian psychiatrist Dr. Doidge advises we carefully select what we listen to and the experiences in which we participate because:

> *While the human brain has apparently underestimated itself, neuroplasticity [our brain's ability to establish new neural pathways in response to learning or through experience] isn't all good news; it renders our brains not only more resourceful but also more vulnerable to outside influences.*

As a young adult, when I listened to loud and rebellious music, I noticed it made me aggressive and disrespectful of others. Now I feel my energy being drained when the music coming from the vehicle next to me is so loud it vibrates my car.

A friend recently picked me up, and the radio in her car was so loud I couldn't hear a word she was saying. I asked her to turn it down. She said, "Sorry, I did not notice."

We are becoming accustomed to too much noise. Constant or loud noises cause us to feel stressed and angry, and they cause us to detach from what is happening in the present, like my friend who did not notice her radio volume. We need to protect ourselves from excessive noise.

The same is true of our being impacted by steady streams of negative news and opinionated commentary. With the current news trend of having commentators reduce complex global issues to cynical, dualistic arguments, it is easy to develop an attitude that's apathetic and fearful of a gloomy world. There is a difference between responsibly staying informed and allowing ourselves to be swallowed up by negativity.

Someone I know became addicted to television court dramas—so much so that she experienced frequent panic attacks and no longer found value in her daily life. Her relationships suffered, and she gained a tremendous amount of weight from eating while glued to the endless spectacle as it unfolded daily over the television.

Murder trials, civil suits, conflict, and other examples of corrupted and negative behavior have existed for centuries. What has not existed until the past several decades is our being constantly exposed, in graphic detail, to the horrible actions of the immoral and unconscious.

To lead with our heart, we determine how watching people treat each other badly can possibly support us in establishing mutually rewarding relationships. How does being constantly exposed to violence, sex, and financial and ethical misconduct contribute to our happiness, peace, and personal responsibility? How does being assaulted by steady pessimism allow us to create optimistic lives? How does continuously subjecting ourselves to violent video games promote peace, empathy, and understanding? How does reliance on the opinion of others allow us to make informed decisions based on fact and truth? How does listening to messages of blame, fear, hate, and divisiveness aid in our arriving at win-win solutions for the challenges we face as a human family?

It is our heart-responsibility to pay attention to what we expose ourselves to. Let us become mindful so we do not let ourselves be influenced by negative, unrealistic, and untrue ideas of what we should be, what our lives should look like, and what should make us happy.

We can start by questioning how the messages we are exposed to impact our worldview. Pay close attention to what is emotionally intrusive and what makes you physically uncomfortable. Notice your stress level when you are exposed to negative editorial commentary or are listening to loud, violent, or denigrating music, television, or video games.

Leading with your heart requires stepping into the role of responsible gatekeeper to what you allow in. Remember too that you are not intended to be a slave to technology. If you find yourself setting aside personal interactions and interpersonal communication in favor of gadgets, it means technology is no longer working for you, and perhaps you need to reassess your relationship with it. And if all else fails, there is always an off switch.

Satisfaction and joy come from creating deep, lasting relationships with ourselves and others. Accomplishing this requires developing the peaceful, purposeful presence that comes from controlling what we allow in and what we allow to distract us from what is happening in the moment. You and I can develop the patience and self-control necessary to manage technology and distractions.

We turn off the cell phone when sitting across the table from family and friends and immerse ourselves fully in the conversation at hand. When the people in our lives want to share how their day was, we choose to turn off the television. We place more value on listening attentively and fully acknowledging their joy and excitement with life. When we drive, we choose to concentrate completely on the road and other drivers. We place greater value on keeping ourselves and others safe by waiting for an appropriate time to text, eat, or talk on the phone.

To successfully navigate our attention-deficit world, we think about an axiom every carpenter values: Slow down to patiently measure twice and cut once. That means we concentrate fully on the most important task at hand. Single-tasking, or finishing what we are engaged with in the moment before moving on to the next item, actually allows us to speed up. Completing something right the first time we do it beats wasting time putting out fires that result from sloppiness or miscommunication.

STAYING PRESENT IN THE NOW

According to Merriam-Webster's dictionary, *peruse* means "to examine or consider with attention and in detail." And dictionary.com says *peruse* means "to read through with thoroughness or care."

Have you thought about what a difference it would make to your peace and joy if you actually perused life rather than skimming through it? One day, I asked myself this question. Stressed and hurried, I felt disconnected from myself and life. Why was I constantly choosing to experience life as if I were a stone tossed out across a lake, touching down then skipping above the water, over and over? The moments when I was above the water, or the present, far outweighed the times I was immersed in whatever I was doing.

When I consciously slowed down, I became introspective. I asked myself, "Regina, if you are not devoted to patiently immersing yourself fully in the here and now, how is it possible for you to actually enjoy life? Where is the satisfaction in allow-ing your thoughts to fantasize about a future event, rather than staying present to listen closely to a friend? What joy do you receive from letting your thoughts return you to a past situation, instead of patiently remaining present to thoroughly read and comprehend an e-mail from a relative? Why waste time wanting a traffic jam to be different?"

The past is no longer a real moment in time that we can influence or change. The past only holds memories of our life as it was. Returning to fond memories brings us great joy, but the past officially ended the instant we stepped from the then into now.

We cannot go back in time to change the choices we made. Reflecting on the past and our previous choices is the way we learn. Allowing our mind to dwell on what we think should have, would have, or could have been takes our attention away from the present. Only in the present is it possible to apply what we learned from the past and create a better outcome for the moment that is now.

The same is true of the future. Regardless of how badly we may want the future to come, we cannot rush ahead and live in a time that does not yet exist. The future is not real; it is only the next moment's present, over and over, infinitely.

Permitting our mind to race ahead and attach itself to wor-ries of what may happen disconnects us from the present, the only time possible to purposefully get ready for a future event. Living a fulfilled life requires us to patiently surrender to the truth: Life is only real now.

You and I have a conscious choice to make. We can live dis-connected from the present while convincing ourselves that we are actually plugged in, or we can slow down, remain patient, and focus our attention on immersing ourselves in the moment at hand. One truth is that there is something wonderful hidden in every moment of life. Another is that our contentment comes from slowing down to find it.

MEDITATIONS AND EXERCISES

Sit down in a quiet place and write down your answers to these questions:

1. Have you ever had an accident as a result of multitasking, such as talking on the phone or texting while driving? Was there negative fallout as a result?

2. Have you recently tried single-tasking? What was the outcome when you completed one thing before moving on to another?

3. What keeps you from living right here, right now, fully in the present moment? How might you eliminate or limit those distractions?

Remaining present is not as difficult as it may seem, but it does take deliberate effort and commitment. It takes being responsible for when and where our mind wanders.

Here are a couple exercises that will help you to stay in the present moment and focus:

1. When you find yourself distracted, hurried, stressed, or feeling out of sync with life, pause. Take a deep breath, and take time to connect with your thoughts. Slow down. Focusing on your thoughts returns your attention to the real life that is happening right in front of you. You will discover a difference in the overall quality of your life when you are devoted to honoring your present. Patiently immerse yourself in it and pay attention to the here and now.

2. You can choose not to buy into the multitasking myth. You can be responsible for getting to the heart of the matter by limiting distractions to keep your attention focused on what is most important in life—safety, family, friends, peace, joy, clear communication, expressing emotions, and leading with your heart. At your next family meal, turn off the television and all cell phones. It may be uncomfortable at first, but notice what sort of interaction transpires. Or, in the morning, wait one full hour before checking e-mails or going on the Internet. Take this extra time to plan your day. At night, go to bed with a good book instead of your laptop.

NOTES

Communicate with Care

When I was sixteen years old, I learned a hard lesson. I remember it as if it were yesterday. The midsummer evening was a bit cooler than average for that time of year in south Texas. A beautiful, red-orange sunset filled the horizon. Dragonflies were out in force helping to keep swarms of hungry mosquitoes at bay. It seemed the perfect night for a competitive yet friendly game of softball with the girls from the Devereux team.

My friend Debbie and I were playing catch before the game. She accidently threw the ball over my head. As I turned to race after it, I said, "Debbie, you dummy."

Debbie was not offended. She knew I was kidding. We were good friends on and off the field. We laughed and joked. This time was no different, and I had no clue my picture-perfect evening was about to turn ugly.

Throughout the next nine innings, the girls on the opposing team repeatedly called me bad names and taunted me. They said I was stupid, ugly, and dumb. I was distraught, desperate to comprehend the reason. They were not treating any of my team members rudely. I could not fathom why the girls, many of whom I thought of as friends, had singled me out for ridicule and verbal abuse.

The Deveraux players tried to run into me when they rounded second base. They angrily heckled me at bat. When I was on base, they continued shouting mean things at me from the dugout.

Their words hurt, and their behavior was confusing, beyond the teenage competitive rivalry to which I was accustomed. I was at a complete loss until after the game, when one of their team members approached me and angrily said, "Don't you ever call the Devereux team dummies again!"

Suddenly the events of the evening made sense. When we were warming up, someone on their team must have misheard what I said to Debbie. Instead of hearing, "Debbie, you dummy," she probably heard, "Devereux is a dummy." What she thought she heard spread throughout the entire team.

My heart broke a little more. While many people may not think calling someone a dummy is a big insult, I knew how sensitive the girls were. As residents of Devereux, they were part of a treatment program for people with a wide range of emotional, behavioral, developmental, and chemical dependency issues. It upset me deeply to think they thought I had purposely said something hurtful.

After many tears and repeated attempts, I eventually convinced some of them I had been misunderstood. Others remained certain I had deliberately insulted them.

Our individual experiences and perceptions weigh heavily on how we interpret information. I discovered that while it is not possible to control what other people hear, it is possible to control what I say. That is my concern.

Although my friend was not offended by my calling her a dummy, I credit the distress of being misheard as the point in my life when I became more careful about what I said to other people. Since that night on the ball field, I have done everything in my power to communicate clearly so there is less chance of being misheard.

On a related note, I went on to learn that cultural differences can also cause innocent and well-meaning communication to be misunderstood. At the Michigan Womyn's Music Festival one year, my band had finished our set and we were backstage listening to other acts. A young woman from Europe was scheduled to perform next. The moment she began to sing, I knew she was destined for stardom.

Moved by her performance, I commented out loud to no one in particular, "She is precious." She was highly skilled, her stage presence was sweet, and the simultaneously innocent and worldly lyrics of her original songs were poetry. She seemed dear standing alone, in full command of the stage.

"What did you call her?" an annoyed voice asked.

Looking over my shoulder, I noticed a woman staring at me. When I met her gaze, she said, "I am her manager, and she is not precious."

"I am sorry, I do not understand," I said. "Precious is a compliment."

"Well, it is not where we come from. To us, calling someone 'precious' is saying they are conceited, arrogant, and pompous!"

Feeling attacked, I immediately wanted to walk away. Instead of getting defensive and reacting, however, I hung in there—not to prove myself "right," but rather to clear up the confusion. In my culture, I had given the young woman on stage a compliment. Apparently this did not hold true for everyone, everywhere.

Owning what I said, without blaming her or making her wrong, I shared with the manager what calling someone precious meant to me. As she shared with me, I understood her point of view, appreciating why she initially got defensive. Her feelings were real based on her cultural experiences.

Her conveying that she felt insulted allowed me to empathize with her. My communicating that I was giving the artist a genuine compliment allowed her a new insight, too.

After a few more exchanges, the woman and I parted on good terms. It was a great lesson in the power of communicating carefully to create shared awareness. Owning our experiences, putting ourselves in each other's shoes, not giving up, and remaining respectful throughout the process allowed us to learn something new about one another's culture.

The backstage incident helped me become more aware of other people's feelings and our different customs. It helped me remain aware that the last thing I want to do is insult someone, including myself.

I once worked for the Robert T. Smith Company, Inc., in Birmingham, Alabama. Mr. Smith was a kind man I greatly admired. Although he had turned over the daily management of his company to others several years earlier, he was on site a few hours each morning, and then off to the golf course in the afternoon.

Mr. Smith had a private office, but he also had another desk, close to mine, in the reception area. One day he arrived to find me with my head buried in my hands. I was sick and felt horrible. He approached and asked how I was.

At the time, I did not consistently think before I spoke. I did not stop to consider the impact of my words. Too often I just opened my mouth and let anything come out. Without realizing what I was about to say, I fired off, "I feel like pounded goat snot."

At first he did not say anything; he just stared at me with a look of stunned disbelief. After what seemed an eternity, he said, "That is the most disgusting thing I believe I've ever heard anybody say."

I was mortified. I truly admired him and cared about what he thought of me. I wanted to crawl under my desk and disappear, or escape unnoticed through the back door. I was bright red with embarrassment.

"Regina, the words you choose to express yourself define you, not only to you but also to the world. What you said was gauche and beneath you," he said. I felt scolded as if I were a child. After looking up *gauche* in the dictionary, I knew he was right.

I often used bad language without consideration. Until I got called out on my "goat snot" comment, I somehow justified occasional tasteless language as cool. I thought it made me part of the in crowd, or that it better emphasized the point I was attempting to make. In reality, cursing or using crass language actually defined me as uncouth, vulgar, and unrefined, no matter who else chose to do it.

I am grateful to Mr. Smith for his patience and caring. He was an elegant man who challenged me to care about how my words painted a picture of me. What I say and how I say it are clear indications of the true value I place on myself.

Mr. Smith's polite reprimand opened a new level of awareness in me of the importance of carefully choosing how I express myself. In a way, my embarrassing interaction with him helped me to be more receptive to, and take advantage of, another major communication realization.

On some level, I knew nonverbal behavior played an important role in communication. When someone rolled their eyes at me, stood with their arms crossed, or put their hands on their hips, I felt their meaning. It wasn't until I was pursuing my master's degree that I really began thinking critically about the role nonverbal cues play in all areas of life.

The research for a paper I was writing on communication shocked me. I learned that words only constitute about 7 percent of our interactions. How we say what we do, through the volume, pitch, and rhythm of our voice, accounts for about 38 percent. The remaining 55 percent consists of the silent body messages we send. This makes it vital to pay close attention to what our nonverbal behavior conveys to others.

Two women were walking across the street while I was stopped in the left turn lane at a traffic light. Suddenly one of them shouted at me, "Stop moving forward, we are walking here!"

Insulted, I reacted defensively, without thinking, and said, "I am not moving. I am stopped. See!"

"You are stopped now, but you were moving into the cross-walk," she said. "Be more careful next time."

For the rest of the afternoon, I was upset with the woman for accusing me of something I did not think I had done. Being wrongly accused was familiar and painful territory. Yet in all honesty, the woman was probably right. It got me thinking about how it felt to be on the other end of inconsiderate driving behavior.

As I began paying closer attention to my actions, I started leaving adequate space between myself and the car in front of me, so the other driver would not feel I was tailgating—the dangerous, nonverbal equivalent of rushing and pushiness. I became more aware of the silent message I sent when I walked slowly across an intersection while drivers were waiting for me to cross. I also began caring about the selfish message I conveyed when I honked at someone to express my impatience or frustration.

Driving, maneuvering my shopping cart in a store, and my nonverbal communication as a pedestrian all became more important to me, as did being more aware of my facial expressions, tone of voice, and body language. My face communicates my emotions. Sadness, pleasure, or disgust—my face does not lie. My eyes are a dead giveaway, clearly expressing joy, anger, or confusion.

I became more attentive to how my body creates a feeling of either openness or rejection. What does my body express when my arms are crossed while I listen to someone talk? Does the tone of my voice accurately convey my feelings? How does another person feel about shaking my extended hand when my palm is down, instead of up? Do other people feel I am more receptive to their words when I sit upright, slightly leaning in, with my hands loosely folded on my lap?

By remaining aware of the body language of other people, I

began learning about the signals we constantly give. With time, I amassed an internal reference guide giving me clear cues about others. My ability to sense what other people are feeling by observing their nonverbal communication allows me to value the importance of staying connected to the way my body speaks for me.

I credit my good friend for giving me the nonverbal signal of annoyance as the wake-up call I needed to learn about another important aspect of communicating successfully. With fists firmly planted on his hips and a look of frustration on his face, he said, "Regina, stop interrupting. You need to learn to listen!"

When I was growing up, I heard this all the time. It was not until my thirties that my best friend's aggravation prompted me to perceive the truth: I did not listen with the attention necessary to actually hear what was said. His body language and facial expression were just what I needed to finally get it.

In my interactions with people, I thought I was listening, but in reality I was busy talking, being distracted, interrupting, or forming a response while the other person was speaking. It was especially noticeable during heated situations, when it became nearly impossible for me to listen without jumping in to defend myself.

My friend brought my deficient listening skills to my attention, teaching me how to listen. He was fascinating, a walking library of information about many things. Regardless of the topic, I was hooked on each word he shared. During our daily front porch meetings, I learned listening is more than hearing what is being said. Truly listening to another person is establishing an emotional connection with the person talking.

Next to the importance nonverbal cues play, this realization about listening was the communication aha moment that changed my life. Not once had I considered listening as a way to connect and sympathize with another human being. What a wonderful realization.

To really identify with other people, I needed to develop the habit of hearing them with patient acceptance and respect. This became especially important when we discussed contentious topics.

The conversations I had with my friend taught me that high levels of concentration and energy are essential to recognize the value of another person's point of view. I had to set aside my own thoughts and agenda and put myself in his shoes. That meant quieting the ever-present cycle of hearing a critical internal dialogue, forming a response, and waiting to interrupt. To keep my mouth shut and my mind quiet, I concentrated on hearing and feeling what my friend said with my mind and in my heart as he was speaking.

When a conversation became a bit heated, instead of bringing up past conflicts, I remained focused on the current disagreement. I learned to own my position by using "I" statements instead of blaming the other person with "you" statements. No matter how uncomfortable it was, I did not give up. I kept sharing and listening.

I am grateful to my friend for showing me that I needed to learn the art of active listening. Whether in a business meeting, a workshop with dozens of people, or one-on-one over the phone, I now listen quietly to the person who is speaking. Being attentive conveys that what the person is saying is important to me. Respectful listening is giving someone my full attention—without watching TV, reading, texting, talking on the phone, or working on the computer, and without formulating a response while he or she is talking.

Learning to listen also helped me be a better writer and speaker. While listening is a way to recognize other people, writing and speaking are the ways in which I convey the messages I want other people to comprehend.

The goal is to convey information in a clear and concise manner. This is especially important when much of communication today is through depersonalized means, such as e-mail and texting. Although convenient, these methods can easily result in confusion and inefficient communication.

When using impersonal methods of communication, I keep it simple and clear. What I want to say may seem obvious to me, but that does not mean the person I am communicating with will be able to accurately fill in the blanks if I leave things out. People cannot read my mind or hear what I intend. Being clear is my responsibility. Consequently, when writing any communication, I focus on leaving no room for misinterpretation or misunderstanding.

Each time I speak, I remember Mr. Smith's lesson to choose my words carefully. Remaining connected to and responsible for what I am saying while I am saying it, I keep my language clean, respectful, and polite. Class or crass, the choice is mine.

Looking back, I am grateful for each painful and embarrassing lesson that helped me learn to communicate with care. As a result, my relationships have flourished.

Each day we interact with people who have different experiences, perceptions, cultures, and beliefs from ours. While it is not possible to control what other people hear, it is possible to control what we say about others and ourselves. While we cannot make other people listen to us, we can choose to listen respectfully to others, with a quiet mind and mouth. We can remain aware of our body language and other nonverbal messages we constantly send to other people. We can pay attention to ensure our written communication is clear and complete.

Communication defines us to ourselves and to the world. How we communicate sets the stage for the relationships we have. It is amazing how much our self-image and the interactions we have with others improve when we assume responsibility for communicating with care, by speaking as we want to be spoken to and listening as we want to be heard.

MEDITATIONS AND EXERCISES

Our relationships are the most important and fulfilling aspect of the lives we create. A key ingredient in deep relationships is productive communication. Clear, stress-free, honest sharing and receiving of information builds trust and mutual respect, and establishes support and intimacy. Learning to speak as we want to be spoken to and listen as we want to be heard is important, because communication is a more complex and error-prone process than many of us may realize.

To begin to learn better communication, write down your answers to the following questions:

1. Do you rely on texting and e-mail as a primary method of communicating with others?

2. Has something you've written by text or e-mail ever been received in a way you did not intend? What were the results?

3. How would other people describe your communication style? How might you become more aware of the non-verbal signals you send?

4. How does it make you feel when you hear offensive language? Have you ever laughed at a joke that was racist, sexist, or homophobic? What might you have done to change the topic or even express your discomfort?

Here is an exercise that will help you become a better communicator:

For a change, try phoning or handwriting a letter to family or friends. Or, if you're at work, try walking down the hall and speaking face-to-face with your colleague. How does it feel? Does it make you feel impatient or anxious? Why? How does the quality of communication differ?

Tip: As you speak, hear your words in your head and in your heart. When listening to others, hear their words in your head and in your heart. Allow someone to finish speaking before you jump in so you do not interrupt them or make them feel crowded or cut off. Listen to others with a quiet mind, without thinking about a response.

To become more familiar with your nonverbal cues, stand in front of a mirror. Smile, frown, cross your arms, put your hands on your hips, scowl, make a surprised face. Notice how each of these nonverbal actions makes you feel, so you realize how they feel to other people.

 NOTES

Forgive and Move On

As a young child, I got very sick. My mom took me to the doctor, where he and his nurse mistakenly used an adult catheter. I screamed and screamed and tried desperately to pull it out. They ignored my screams, perhaps because I was so young. They only realized the mistake after the fact. My mother was upset, but neither she nor the medical staff could take back what was already done.

I knew from a young age I was different—gay. I quickly found that the place intended to provide an accepting, loving, and supportive haven for everyone—my fundamentalist Christian church in Texas—actually did not. "Love your neighbor as yourself" only seemed to apply if that neighbor met a list of predetermined criteria. Attempting to fit in when I was already deemed unworthy became a recipe for anger and emotional chaos.

Around age eleven, my sixteen-year-old male babysitter molested me. He said, "I'll cut your tits off if you ever tell anyone what I am doing." I was terrified. He was the son of one of our neighbors. Since I was forced to see him often, I felt completely powerless. I had to keep the secret, unable to expose him or to ask for protection.

When I was seventeen, a physician casually ordered his nurse to leave the room so he could molest me in private. He justified his actions as part of the examination. But I knew he was touching me inappropriately.

These are four examples over the course of my life of times I've been deeply hurt or betrayed by the actions of others. For years I held on to the pain of being let down, ridiculed, bullied, slandered, persecuted, and abused. A continuous loop of negative memories played in my mind, keeping me shackled to a suitcase of blame and resentment for the unjust mistreatment. Each day I grew angrier and more self-destructive from holding on to what I thought the people who hurt me should have done differently.

Refusing to let go of the fantasy of what could have been was like endlessly tearing a scab off a wound, preventing it from ever healing. I was unhappy and misguided, wandering aimlessly through life without the ability to focus on much else other than the growing list of ways I had been victimized. Perpetuating an angry victim identity caused me to spiral downward into a state of constant annoyance, blame, and a lack of self-respect. I was suffocating under the burden of carrying the indignant displeasure and persistent ill will against those who wronged, insulted, and injured me.

Frustrated and feeling like a prisoner of the past, I finally sought help. I got other people's advice. I went to a counselor. I attended support groups. I looked outside myself for years for the answer to how to heal. Yet no matter who or what I brought in to help, no matter how good the advice, I did not achieve the release I wanted until one day, like a bucket of ice water thrown in my face, the truth opened my eyes. To heal I had to intentionally choose to move on from the past.

No matter what had happened to me back then, I was the one choosing to relive it in the present. It was my choice to keep the hurt and resentment alive by dragging them into each new day. Those who mistreated me had moved on or died or were oblivious to the pain they inflicted. Even if each of them were to emotionally wake up, assume liability for their actions, and beg for my forgiveness, the past would still remain unchanged. What was done was done. I was the one permitting the people who had hurt me in the past to continue having power over me in the present. This aha moment allowed me to wrap my heart around the truth that I was the only one capable of engaging in the actions necessary to change my present circumstances. To have the best rest of my life, I had to take my power back and stop dragging around all that happened back then.

The professional advice I received to move on by concentrating on the present made sense. Yes, I needed to stay present in the now to enjoy life. But it was not possible until the constant negative mind chatter that kept me reliving the past was under control.

I began retaking control of my mind by honestly confronting the events of my past and quieting the negative mind chatter that plagued me. No more gliding over the truth or shoving it out of my mind as fast as possible. I intentionally went back and addressed each painful event not as a victim, but as a powerful adult who was now able to support the child and young girl who had endured the mistreatment.

My healing began in earnest when I realized the young Regina who was hurt did not have the skills to heal the adult I was today. It was the adult Regina who was stronger, kinder, and more responsible than the people and circumstances that hurt me. It was the adult Regina who understood people who hurt others are emotionally oblivious to the pain and suffering they cause. It was the adult me who chose to forgive to move on. But first, I had to determine what it actually meant to forgive.

FORGIVING OTHERS

According to dictionary.com, to forgive is to: grant pardon for or remission of (an offense, debt, etc.); absolve; cancel an indebtedness or liability of; and cease to feel resentment.

How would it be possible for me to absolve the people who had hurt me of liability for the pain and heartbreak they caused? Wasn't letting them off the hook by exonerating their actions basically condoning their behavior? I could not imagine anyone excusing mistreatment. And, careless mistakes still hurt, though unintentional errors are easier to release with the acceptance that no one is perfect.

While I now see the abusive behavior of the people in my past was unconscious and self-centered, does that release them from accountability? Ignorance of the law does not mean we have a free pass to behave as we please; why should it be any different with social contracts? The physician and babysitter were certainly aware of the legal and societal consequences of their actions.

The babysitter's threat meant he understood what he was doing was unacceptable. But he was motivated by the cruel, egocentric mind-set that intimidating me with the threat of violence would ensure my silence so he would not be caught.

The physician was blinded by his ego. He viewed himself a powerful member of the community, entitled to behave as he pleased. He rationalized that the ethical standards and honorable responsibilities that applied to everyone else in his profession, and to people of good character in general, did not apply to him.

Likewise, those who continue to thoughtlessly perpetuate ancient judgmental beliefs about homosexuality are not, no matter how much they tell themselves they are, emotionally aligned with the axiom "treat others as you want to be treated." They too are blinded by justifications for their prejudice.

Initially, it did not feel right to cancel the liability or indebtedness the people who had hurt me had for the consequences of their actions. It was not like they borrowed money and could not pay me back. The physical, emotional, and mental abuse they inflicted could not be taken back. Imagining the day when the people who betrayed me would own up to their mistreatment was living a dream. Not one of them ever asked for my forgiveness. Their seeming obliviousness to the impact of their actions was frustrating. But the ice-cold bucket of truth remained undeniable.

Regardless of how much I wanted those who hurt me to go

back and make my life right, it was not possible for them, or me, to do so. I could not be paid back, because they could not make right what they did. My clinging to the idea they were indebted to me kept those people and the pain they inflicted fresh. As long as I felt they owed me something, I was waiting for reimbursement. I did not want them or the negative memories of mistreatment to dominate my life any longer.

To forgive, I had to intentionally bypass the beliefs of my mind and what I thought should happen, and accept with my heart that the people who hurt me were actually emotionally oblivious to the outcome of their actions. My aha moment— the recognition that people who mistreat, persecute, and abuse others are emotionally unaware—allowed me to wrap my heart around the healing truth in the words of author and poet Maya Angelou, "When you know better you do better."

For too long I justified staying angry with people because I thought anyone who hurt me should "know" better, because I knew their mistreatment and abuse were not right. That people should know better was a lie of my wounded, angry ego. Simply because we know better does not mean other people do or have the emotional awareness necessary to control their actions.

Over the course of my life, I've done many things I am not proud of. I knew stealing twenty dollars out of my dad's wallet was wrong, but I did it anyway. One day I woke up emotionally. I put myself in his position and questioned how it would feel to have money stolen from me. Asking "how would it feel?" connected me to a new level of acceptance that I am personally responsible for the consequences of not controlling my actions.

For me, stealing is a big issue and wrong. For other people, stealing is wrong but still thought of as acceptable behavior.

So yes, those who abuse others comprehend, intellectually, that their behavior is wrong, and in most cases illegal and immoral. But no, they do not realize with emotional conscious-ness, which would enable the sensitivity of their heart to over-rule the rationalizations of their egocentric mind in order to control their behavior.

When people are cut off from the emotional responsibility of their heart, ego takes over, with endless justifications and ratio-nalizations for negative, thoughtless, and self-centered behav-ior. It takes sensitive awareness to remain connected to and responsible for the way our actions impact other people and all life. That is how we distinguish when people have emotionally awakened: when we see that they are no longer blind to their impact on others. They begin seeing themselves in other people and other forms of life, and caring for them.

If you are currently in an abusive situation, you must set a boundary with people who hurt you. Choose to respect yourself and walk away, if necessary. No matter how your heart might long for the other person to know better, he or she will not have a clue about their negative behavior until they choose to look at themselves with the honesty of their own heart.

To begin releasing myself from the resentments of the past, I sat down one day, when I was alone and the house was quiet, and made a list of everyone and everything I could remember that hurt. Then I transcribed each person or circumstance onto a small piece of paper. In the end, my table was covered with pieces of paper. Gathering them into a bag, I went to my back-yard. I took the papers out of the bag and read the words written on each. One by one, I set them on fire.

As I dropped each safely into an old clay plant saucer, I repeated, "I accept this happened and that it is okay to be angry. I also accept I cannot do anything to change you or the past. Your behavior was not my fault, and I am not condoning your actions. By forgiving, I no longer allow you the power to continue hurting me. I am reclaiming power over my life and my thoughts. You are no longer welcome on my journey."

I forgave myself for believing the lies other people told me about me: I was stupid, unworthy, going to hell, ugly, etc. I realized none of these was ever true. People said and did hurtful things because they were hurting or unconscious and projected their pain, fear, and insecurity onto me.

As I watched the smoke rise, I felt the weight of resentment being lifted. No matter how horrible I judged what had happened to me, the reality was that I did come out a better person for having gone through what I did.

Abusive, unconscious people taught me acceptance, support, compassion, and to question my thoughts and beliefs about myself and others. My forgiving brought a higher level of self-awareness than what created the mistreatment in the first place. Forgiveness turned over the pages of my past so I began life anew on the clean page that is *now*. Forgiveness is one of the ways I demonstrate self-love and respect.

The haunting memories of my past did not magically go away with the backyard ceremony. Flashes of events continue to this day. I do not believe it reasonable to think forgiveness permanently erases our memories. Yet, over time, with purposeful attention, we can retrain ourselves to allow a memory to come in and go out without emotionally attaching any significance to it. Each time a memory comes up, I mentally say, "You have no power over me. I have forgiven and released you." Addressing your thoughts this way keeps you from attaching to and getting stuck reliving them.

Whether you are haunted by financial difficulties, divorce, sexual violations, betrayal, the death of a family member, infidelity, or abuse, or receiving a traffic ticket, you cannot change what happened by keeping your focus on the event. Wanting a situation to be different from the way it is causes you to be trapped in a cycle of anger, depression, hopelessness, victimization, and desire for revenge. It can make you give up on life.

When you choose to respond to life's challenges with forgiveness, the bitterness and desire to assign blame vanish. Forgiveness helps heal emotional wounds so you do not inappropriately take your baggage out on those you say you love, or the strangers you meet each day. Forgiveness is truly the only way to take back your power from those who abused, judged, or ridiculed you.

No one remains untouched by unpleasant situations. Life comes with challenges. Suffering over the past does not allow us to live today. Forgiveness does.

Regardless of what happened in your past, even if that is yesterday, releasing resentment and what you think should have been is the key that unlocks the door to your freedom. Bitterness and judgment are emotions that hurt you, not the people who inflicted their unconsciousness onto you. For your physical, mental, emotional, and spiritual well-being, let go of what happened so you can create today on your terms.

FORGIVING YOURSELF

Forgiving yourself is just as important as forgiving others. Withholding forgiveness of yourself also denies you peace. To be free of self-resentment, you recognize that holding on to whatever you did to other people only perpetuates your pain.

Over the course of my life, I spent a lot of time beating myself up for the mistakes and bad choices I made until one experience in particular taught me that no amount of guilt or remorse has the power to undo what has already been done. And forgiving myself does not mean I disregard what I did.

While attending Sam Houston State University, I was on the softball team. One day, a team member shared something in confidence with me. Although I assured her I was going to keep her secret safe, I chose to tell someone. It did not take long for my indiscretion to return to her. Regardless of what I said to excuse, rationalize, or apologize for betraying her trust, she refused to listen.

At practice and during games, she avoided me. Soon other players learned of my bad decision and stayed away from me as well. I was devastated. My ability on the softball field plummeted, and I was benched. My grades fell, too.

It was impossible for me to forget what I did. Tossing and turning, I was unable to sleep. Filled with remorse, I relentlessly punished myself, wasting countless hours dreaming of ways to take back what I did. I was willing to do anything for my teammate's forgiveness, but she refused to talk to me.

It felt horrible to keep beating myself up for a past mistake. I wanted to move on, yet how was that possible if she did not forgive me? I had apologized, and in my heart I was genuinely sorry. Still she flatly refused to forgive. In order to move on I had to forgive myself, and that meant learning from the experience so I would not make the same mistake again.

The next time I was in a position to gossip or betray another person, I refused to do so. Making a different, better choice was the only way possible to make amends to myself, and in an indirect way to the woman I hurt. At last I felt free of guilt and disappointment. I was finally able to sleep. Remorse no longer dominated my thoughts. It was then I realized no amount of beating me up actually changed what had happened. Feeling miserable motivated me to not want to feel that way again. Therefore, I began purposely paying close attention to the possible consequences of my actions before acting, in order to avoid making thoughtless mistakes and having to experience the horrible feelings of self-loathing and disrespect that resulted.

Regardless of how large or small the infractions, spending time regretting your bad choices does not change them. The only way to redeem yourself in your heart, even if you are not forgiven by others or your bad choice results in being punished by society, is not to repeat the offense again.

Life is a series of choices. Often we make careless, hasty, or selfish choices that negatively impact us and other people. No matter what we did to ourselves or other people, we close the door on regret by releasing what we think should, would, or could be. We are completely honest with ourselves and others about our behavior. We apologize to those we hurt and truly mean it. Whether our apology is accepted or not, we let go of the past. We move on by changing negative behavior aimed at revenge against others to positive behavior, which supports us. We let go of wanting to change the past. We stop letting past choices define our present. We step up to deal positively with past, uncomfortable situations of life and unpleasant, critical people.

Our overall contentment with life is dependent upon rising to meet life's challenges with the best of ourselves during the worst of times. Being our best includes forgiving ourselves and others, healing, and moving on.

MEDITATIONS AND EXERCISES

Why does it seem so hard to forgive, heal, and move on? Once you make the decision to stop seeing yourself as a victim, you learn it is not as hard as you keep telling yourself it is. To begin the healing, ask yourself these questions:

1. What past events have you allowed to negatively impact your present?
2. What forgiveness can you offer yourself?
3. What forgiveness can you offer to others?

4. How do you think it would feel to let go of wishing you could change a mistake you made, and instead concentrate on making a better choice in the future?

5. Have you considered that fully embracing your past is the way to fully release it?

To ponder: Life is not as complicated as we make it. Healing is not as hard as it might seem. It is possible to be continuously satisfied, and to strive to do the right thing without feeling burdened or mentally exhausted. Changing a negative habit takes time and practice, but it is not as hard as you make it. The key to accomplishing all of these things is your attitude: you can do absolutely whatever you want. To be successful, you must get out of your own way. And it's okay to think about giving up sometimes—so long as you don't follow through on it.

Here is an exercise that will help you to forgive:

Go to a quiet, comfortable, and safe place where you will not be interrupted. Think back to the times when you were hurt by the actions of others. Write each instance on a separate sheet of paper. When you are finished, put them into a bag.

Find a safe place to burn the papers, such as a fireplace, outdoor grill, fire pit, or a clay saucer that is placed on a concrete or dirt surface away from things like leaves or dry grass. As a precaution, have a bottle or two of water handy.

Take one paper out of the bag, and read what you have written. Remember the event, not as a victim of it, but as the powerful person you are now. Feel whatever emotions and feelings naturally come up. Then imagine you are a colander, and allow your emotional attachments to that event of your past to pour out and wash away.

Once you have felt the memories of this event, light the piece of paper on fire, and envision the pain of that event being burned up. See the person who hurt you standing in front of you. As the smoke rises from the paper, envision that any anger and resentment you still carry toward him or her are rising, leaving with the smoke.

I welcome you to repeat the same release affirmation I used, or you can write your own: "I accept this happened and that it is okay to be angry. I also accept I cannot do anything to change you or the past. Your behavior was not my fault, and I am not condoning your actions. By forgiving, I no longer allow you the power to continue hurting me. I am reclaiming power over my life and my thoughts. You are no longer welcome on my journey."

Repeat this process with the other pieces of paper, until you've worked through and released all of the pain from your past.

NOTES

Body

I have to be honest—I don't like to exercise. I'd rather have toned muscles, a flat stomach, and cardiovascular health magically by eating cheeseburgers, french fries, and pizza, and sitting on the couch watching TV. But I tried the "do nothing and eat everything" diet, and for some reason it didn't work. So I force myself to go to the gym and work out, because while I don't like exercise, I love what regular physical activity and eating healthy do for me. I feel better, sleep better, am hardly ever sick, and the last time I went to my doctor he said, "You look great!"

You only get one body. To ensure it stays healthy and fit requires taking care of it on a daily basis. Watching what you eat and getting regular exercise and adequate sleep are a few of the ways to nurture your body. Spending time in the natural world helps you eliminate stress and deepens your connection to all life. Since your outer environment is a reflection of your inner life, it is vital to maintain clean spaces to limit distractions and the unnecessary anxiety that comes from clutter. And making time to play gives your mind, body, and spirit some much-needed downtime to relax and refresh.

Nurture Your Body

At this point in my life, I honestly have no regrets. There is absolutely no way to go back and change anything I did or did not do in the past. My only power is to learn from previous negative choices and not repeat them. Yet, if a magic wand suddenly appeared and made it possible to do a part of life over again, I would jump at the chance to consciously nurture my body each day.

Too many years of lifting and carrying heavy objects weakened my back, resulting in two surgeries. With nerve damage it was challenging to exercise, and I was not motivated. For too long I simply chose to ignore that I was overeating. Today I realize I was attempting to medicate away the pain and disappointment over my impaired body with food. But eating without awareness caused me to gain so much weight that I did not recognize myself in the mirror.

One day, I bravely faced my fear and honestly looked at myself in the mirror. With tears in my eyes, I managed to see past the overweight stranger and into my heart. No matter how I abused my body, the spark of life that made Regina Victoria Cates was still alive.

It was not possible to change the past or undo what neglect and feelings of unworthiness had done to my body. The only option was to accept that the rest of my life lay before me. Then and there, I decided to love myself by taking my body back for good.

Since I allowed myself to be distracted by other activities, I was unaware of how much I actually ate. To lose the amount of weight I wanted required me to stay emotionally present with my eating and carefully count calories. No more watching television, driving, or reading during dinner. I began eating responsibly.

Walking in my neighborhood each day eased me back into regular physical activity. When I got a bit stronger, I bought a bicycle and rode a few miles at a time. Gaining strength and stamina, I joined a gym. After six months of working out two hours a day, six days a week, I lost the first thirty pounds. Riding my mountain bike fifteen miles each day around the beautiful wilderness of Berry College helped me shed another ten pounds.

By eliminating most sugar and all fake sugar substitutes, I lost the last fourteen pounds of extra weight. It also helped get rid of the inflammation that caused me to feel tired all the time and to suffer from joint pain, disease, and overall ill health. Being from the South, I had to pay purposeful attention to stop drinking sodas and sweet tea. Candy, cookies, and sugar in my coffee also went by the wayside. Sweeteners such as stevia and blue agave nectar replaced the sugar in my coffee.

I now stay away from fried foods and limit the amount of white rice, white breads, pastas, and cream sauces I consume. Salads and fruit are my main diet. For health, environmental, and spiritual reasons, I rarely eat red meat.

On rare occasions, I treat myself to an order of french fries, a slice of pizza, or cheese enchiladas covered with raw white onions. Once a month I have a tasty dinner with dessert, during which I do not care about calories.

In addition to conscious eating, exercising three or four times a week has become my new lifestyle. For too many years, I made excuses that there was not enough time in my busy schedule. I no longer do. I am still busy, but making time for regular exercise is a top priority.

Regular physical activity is crucial to my long-term health goal of keeping fit to maintain my active lifestyle. To create the space for it, I happily give up some other activities so I can get six to eight hours of exercise a week. The benefits I receive from this commitment are irreplaceable.

Exercise has been shown to improve mood, boost mental focus, and promote better sleep. A regular exercise program also improves your chances of avoiding Alzheimer's and senility. Physical activity stimulates various brain chemicals, leaving you content, more confident, relaxed, and looking and feeling better overall.

Physical workouts also help prevent chronic conditions such as heart disease. According to the Busy Woman Fitness website, regular physical activity reduces the risk of breast cancer by upwards of 60 percent. Exercise boosts high-density lipoprotein (HDL), or good cholesterol, while decreasing triglycerides. This makes your blood flow more smoothly by lowering the buildup of plaque in arteries and reducing the risk of high blood pressure.

Added to cardiovascular exercise, lifting weights increases bone density. Strength training helps prevent osteoporosis and future stress fractures. Weightlifting increases the metabolism, helps maintain body size, and fights against body fat.

Next to eating healthily and exercising regularly, I drink lots of water. Coffee remains my drink of choice, but water is what makes up almost 60 percent of our body weight. According to the Mayo Clinic, each organ and system in the body depends on water to stay healthy. Water flushes out toxins, carries nutrients to cells, and provides the proper environment for ear, nose, and throat tissues. Water also keeps our skin hydrated.

Another lifestyle change I made for my overall health was getting enough sleep. According to the *Harvard Women's Health Watch*, a monthly newsletter produced by Harvard Medical School, there are several benefits of getting adequate sleep. One is that our brain commits new information to memory when we sleep through a process called memory consolidation. Studies show that people who slept seven to nine hours after learning a new task outperformed those who did not get enough sleep.

Sleep deprivation also causes weight gain and affects the way the body processes and stores carbohydrates. In addition, not enough sleep alters the hormone levels that affect appetite. The newsletter also notes that being sleepy can cause traffic mishaps. I know that when I don't get enough sleep, I become agitated and more prone to stress. Too little sleep also leaves me tired and unable to do the things I enjoy doing.

Sleep disorders have been linked to hypertension, increased stress-hormone levels, and irregular heartbeat. Deprivation of sleep alters the functioning of the immune system, which helps the body fight disease.

Along with conscious eating, exercise, drinking water, and adequate sleep, I get regular health checkups. I visit the dentist two times a year, and I brush and floss my teeth twice a day.

Throughout the day, I focus on breathing deeply, expanding my stomach outward. Each night I spend ten minutes stretching before I go to sleep. Regular vitamin supplements, especially Omega-3s, vitamins C, D, and B, and a good quality multivitamin are a daily routine. A home manicure and pedicure are on my agenda once a week, and each month or so I have a professional manicure and pedicure. To help ensure my body stays aligned, I occasionally visit a chiropractor or get a deep-tissue massage. Meditation is also a vital part of my daily effort to remain physically, emotionally, and spiritually healthy.

I spend a lot of time and money on my body, but I believe the investment is crucial. My physical body is home to my heart (soul). I accept responsibility for not doing the best job of taking care of my body early in life, and now I accept the commitment to care for my body well each day.

Today, my weight is stable. I enjoy physical and cardiovascular fitness. By investing the energy and determination to recover my body, I now have self-respect for choosing to nurture my body with lifestyle changes.

Unlike a house, car, or television, I cannot purchase a new body when the one I have wears out, gets injured, or becomes sick. Although I am now healthy and feel fantastic, I accept the fact that my body will not be the same as before the two back surgeries.

Now that I am doing all that is within my power to make certain my body is loved and cared for, my sights are set on living a long and healthy life. During that time, I want to remain independent. I have no desire to grow older needing assistance to live. While that may happen someday, I am determined to invest the time and energy necessary to make certain I have a great quality of life for as long as possible.

I learned the hard way that invasive actions to my body have consequences. My goal is to avoid the need for drugs or surgery to correct what I am able to prevent with attention and care.

Our body is a magnificent machine designed to last us from birth to death. We live in a time where medical advancements are helping to prolong life, yet the main thing is not how long we live, but rather the quality of the life we live. While many life variables cannot be controlled, it helps our peace of mind to know we are taking each action we can to have the healthiest body possible.

Love yourself by loving your body. Take charge of eating with awareness. Turn off the television and other distractions to stay present with the amount of food you eat. Read the back of food containers for calories, sodium, and preservatives. Avoid processed foods, sugar, fake sugar substitutes, and fast foods. If you can't identify the ingredients that make up what you're eating, don't eat it.

Value the life-enhancing benefits of getting adequate sleep. Drink plenty of water to keep your bodily systems operating at the highest efficiency. Take deep belly breaths throughout the day. Protect yourself from excessive noise and the sun. Research the possible benefits of adding certain vitamin supplements to your diet. Think about yoga as a means of keeping your muscles flexible. If you currently smoke cigarettes, make quitting your top priority. And limit the amount of alcohol you consume.

Each positive action you take to nurture your body today will help ensure the healthiest life possible tomorrow. You are definitely worthy of investing time and energy to improve the health of the body that is home to your heart.

MEDITATIONS AND EXERCISES

Regardless of what physical shape you are in now, and no matter how busy your life, I urge you to make caring for your body a top priority. If you have not seen a physician for a while, get a checkup and create a baseline for a regular program of physical activity.

Sit down in a quiet place and write down your answers to these questions:

1. Do you have a regular fitness routine? Describe it.
2. How many meals do you eat at a fast-food restaurant each week?
3. Do you eat with awareness, watch sugar intake, and check food labels?
4. Do you smoke, drink, or do recreational drugs?
5. Do you get adequate rest, drink plenty of water, and get regular health and dental check-ups?
6. How can you be more nurturing to your body?

Try this exercise to help you remain aware of and grateful for your body:

Sit comfortably with your back straight. Breathe through your nose. Place your right hand on your chest and your left hand on your abdomen, and take a deep breath.

As you inhale, allow your breath to fill your belly. Feel your left hand rise in response to the life-force energy filling your belly. Concentrate on filling your belly so deeply that your left hand, resting on your stomach, moves significantly.

When you exhale, release as much air as possible, contracting your abdominal muscles toward your spine. Your left hand moves inward as you exhale.

Take another breath. Focus attention on filling your lungs, as well as your belly. Feel the air coming in slowly, moving your left hand upward and out as the deepest part of your lungs fill. Exhale and focus on the air moving out through your nose as your lungs and belly relax.

Take another even deeper breath. Be aware of your right hand as your lungs fill. Completely immerse yourself in feeling your body as you take the deepest breath possible. Focus all your attention on filling your lungs and belly with air.

Now take another, even deeper, breath, and hold it. As you exhale, count backwards from ten—ten, nine, eight, seven, six, five, four, three, two, one. Relax your body completely, letting your body breathe fully and naturally.

Your body is grateful for your breath. It needs your breath to keep it animated, healthy, strong, flexible, balanced, peaceful, and alive.

Continue breathing deeply. Stay present and focused on your breathing. If your mind wanders, bring it back to concentrate fully on your breath.

Take another deep breath.

Bring attention to your fingers and hands. Give thanks for your fingers and hands as you imagine holding a glass of cool water.

Take another deep breath.

Bring attention to your arms. Give thanks for your arms as you imagine reaching out to hug a loved one or stroke your pet.

Take another deep breath.

Bring attention to your feet and legs. Give thanks for your feet and legs as they ground you in the present moment and carry you through life.

Take another deep breath.

Bring attention to your internal organs. Give thanks for your heart, lungs, kidneys, all your internal organs, each doing its specific job without being told what to do. Value the inner workings of your body. Your healthy organs keep you vigorous, in balance, moving, and breathing.

Take another deep breath.

Bring attention to your eyes. Give thanks for your eyes as you see your life unfolding in the most joyful way. Be aware of your eyes as they see the beauty that surrounds you.

Take another deep breath.

Bring attention to your ears. Give thanks for your ears that hear your loved ones. Be conscious of your ears, and protect them from loud noises. Tune in to the soft sounds of birds, crickets, rain, and a gentle breeze stirring in the trees.

Take another deep breath.

Bring attention to your nose. Give thanks for your nose as you imagine the fragrance of a rose, or chocolate chip cookies baking in the oven.

Take another deep breath.

Bring attention to your mouth. Give thanks for your mouth as you imagine tasting and savoring your favorite foods.

Take another deep breath.

Bring attention to your skin. Give thanks for your skin, the largest organ of your body, as you imagine the warm sun caressing you or soft sand between your toes as you walk along a peaceful beach.

Take another deep breath.

In this peaceful, relaxed state, think of your body as your best friend. You love your friend, and your friend loves you. Open your heart to care deeply about how your body responds to the air filling your belly and lungs. Feel the warmth of your breath filling your body with love.

Take another deep belly breath and check in with your body. What are you feeling? Are you hungry, tired, hurting? Pay attention. Listen closely. Notice the messages your body sends you. What does your body say?

Take another deep breath.

Listen even more attentively to your body. Your body will tell you what it needs. Honor the information from your body; it does not lie. Take a deep breath and be aware of the positive, protective signals of your body. Love your body by honoring your body's instructions, directions, and guidance.

Take another deep breath.

Make remaining in a balanced, harmonious, centered, and loving place with your body a priority by returning to this exercise frequently.

NOTES

Lead with Your Heart

Appreciate Your Connection to All Life

A gentle thud caught my attention. This sound was curiously familiar. As a bird lover, I realize immediately when one has been temporarily blinded by the sun's reflection, causing it to crash into one of the many windows in my home. I rated this sound similar, yet lighter, reminiscent of one human finger placing a single sharp rap on a pane of glass.

I hurried to the kitchen window that wrapped itself around the right back corner of my house, offering a magnificent view of the tree-filled backyard. Scanning the bushes and grass close to the house, I saw nothing out of the ordinary. I rushed down the steps and reached the bottom just as my border collie, Charlie, who had been roused from a nap by the sound, arrived there. We headed in the same direction, stopping at the hydrangea bushes lining the flower bed beneath the window. There, on a single leaf, lay a hummingbird.

I scooped up the tiny bird before Charlie could get the notion to do it himself, and headed back up the stairs into the safety of the house. Charlie remained there for some time, sniffing for the source of the odd smell that lingered in the air.

Once inside, I opened my hand. Cradled there was one of the most spectacular beauties of Mother Nature, tiny and still. The bird's eyes were shut. It was stunned by the impact, but it was still alive. I saw it breathing, and with one finger pressed lightly against its chest, I felt the rapid beating of its heart.

To get witnesses to this event, I ran next door, braving the likelihood of having to refuse another invitation to tour my aging neighbor's beer bottle collection. On the doorbell's second ring, Marie, the old man's wife, slowly opened the door. Through the screen, she motioned for me to come inside.

"Thanks, Marie, but no. I want you to come outside to see what I have in my hands."

"Robert, come here and see what Regina's got," Marie hollered back over her shoulder into the cavernous hallways of the house.

Soon Robert appeared, smiling from ear to ear, ready with his invitation for the tour. But Marie spoke up before he could.

"Look," she said, pointing to the little mass of metallic green feathers.

"Well, would you look at that," Robert replied. Surprise spread over his face as he saw the tiny bird. He had probably come to greet me with thoughts of familiar things—the weather, how high the grass was growing, and when he'd get around to cutting it. What he found as he opened the screen door to join us on the porch was most likely not in the realm of his imagination. I watched his face as he stepped out into the beautiful spring day. Wrinkles he had borne like badges of honor for all he'd seen during his eighty-five years of life seemed to smooth out in awe of what he now witnessed.

I told them the story and answered their questions as well as I could. When they were satisfied, we all fell silent—a new event in the six years we had known each other.

The bird remained still, its eyes closed as both Marie and Robert took turns gently and lovingly stroking its tiny body. Touching the bird allowed each of us to grasp what we were experiencing as real. It was so soft and downy, small and helpless, yet its powerful heartbeat was proof of its tenacity and will to survive.

After a few more minutes, I told my neighbors goodbye. I felt such a connection with them for sharing the experience with me. But now, something called me to be alone with the little bird. I returned to my front porch and got comfortable in one of the chairs.

I was reluctant to leave it alone, fearing it would become prey to a wandering cat. It was beautiful, small, vulnerable, and yet it displayed a magnificently strong design in such a petite package. I was torn between wanting to keep it and praying for its full recovery.

It was a male ruby-throated, the widest ranging of all North American hummingbirds. I remember as a child growing up in South Texas, they were constant visitors throughout the spring and fall. The tiny bird was common in Central Alabama, too. I often watched three or four competing at my feeder. Almost invisible, they dove, darted, and dive-bombed, and somehow miraculously avoided colliding with each other.

Sitting on the porch holding the bird, I was content. I had witnessed hummingbirds so many times, but never this close. Their wings beat so fast they often seemed more make-believe than real. A blur of color flitting from here to there so quickly my eyes could not follow. Nevertheless, here one was, real and still in the palm of my hand. I was able to study up close the way its little clawed feet curled slightly, and the way its perfectly uniform feathers covered its small body. The vibrant, iridescent colors of its wings and throat were truly amazing.

We sat together for several more minutes. With each moment, I wondered if it was going to make it. Tenderly I stroked its chest, watched, and waited.

Suddenly it woke up. Flipping up from its side, it sprang to life. It hesitated for a split second, seeming to gather its bearings. Then it was off, propelled rapidly upward by its awakening. As it cleared the porch, it made a half-circle and returned to where I was sitting. It hovered in front of me, about two feet from my chair, and remained for what seemed a full minute. Keeping its eyes on me, it stayed back, yet was close enough that I could feel a slight breeze from the rapid beating of its wings. As it looked at me, I thought surely it was saying thanks for plucking it off the leaf and keeping it safe for the past half-hour.

I will not know exactly what the tiny bird was thinking as it made one final circle above my head and flew away. Later I found some feathers on the porch that must have fallen from its wing or tail. They weren't green like its body, or red like its throat, but white and black and gray. Today I still have those feathers in a very special bowl.

Holding the hummingbird was a gift. It was an opportunity that taught me to value the things I love, to cherish each moment, and to courageously get back up when life throws a punch. It was an awesome privilege to be given thirty unforgettable minutes when time stood still and I held the most exquisite creature in my hands, felt its warmth, and marveled at its magnificence.

I have always loved life in all its wonderful forms. I was not the little girl who disliked frogs, snakes, or the curious snail that found a bit of sandwich I had left for the birds. I grew up in love with the splendid variety of life on our beautiful planet, from flowers and trees to lizards and insects to mammals and water creatures. Growing up surrounded by such beauty helped me value the connections among all living things.

The peaceful present bond I feel when I sink my toes into the grass, hang upside down from a low-hanging tree branch, or watch a squirrel stealing seed from my bird feeder makes my heart sing. Each day my passion for the natural world grows stronger, as do my efforts to actively protect it.

You and I are only a single part of life on Earth. When leading with our heart we recognize the value of the wisdom of Chief Seattle:

Humankind has not woven the web of life. We are but one thread within it. Whatever we do to the web, we do to ourselves. All things are bound together. All things are connected.

Our joy and peace are largely dependent upon appreciating our connection to other forms of life. It is healthy for us to regularly spend time in the natural world and to grow in appreciation for our outdoor home. Caring for other people and our natural world is one of the most important heart responsibilities we have.

MEDITATIONS AND EXERCISES

Sit down in a quiet place and write down your answers to these questions:

1. Where are some of your favorite places in the natural world?
2. What do you do to help protect our Earth and other forms of life? Make a list.
3. What emotions come up when you watch animals play, a sun set, a hummingbird drink from a flower, or a butterfly float on the breeze?
4. In your everyday comings and goings, are you aware of insects, animals, and the natural world?

Here is an exercise that will help you connect to nature and all of life:

Devote a part of each day to quietly immersing yourself in the natural world. Allow your mind to become quiet. Let the magnificence of the natural world expand your heart, because what you cherish, you love. What you love, you respect. What you respect, you will protect.

The next time you are alone in your garden, on a hike in the woods, or elsewhere in the natural world, notice your breathing. Notice the muscles in your neck, your chest, your arms, and your legs. What are your thoughts?

How do they differ from your ordinary mind-set? How does the natural world affect you? How are you connected to your surroundings?

Maintain Clean Spaces

As a child, I woke early on Saturday mornings. While the rest of my family slept, I straightened and cleaned the main living areas. It felt more balanced and peaceful to live in a clean environment with things neatly in their place.

Looking back, I see the pleasure I derived from orderliness was partially rooted in the truth that there were many things in my life as a child that I could not control. The things I could control, like keeping my surroundings neat and clean, I did. Yet the delight and peacefulness I felt for having a place for everything and putting everything in its place seemed to have its foundation in something deeper than control.

At the time, I was not familiar with its name. There was only an inner heart-awareness of what I now understand to be the universal flow of energy around and through my body, other people and pets, and the objects surrounding me.

Known in Asian cultures as *qi* (ch'i) or "life-force," this stream of energy is the underlying reason why I feel positive and peaceful when my space is neat and clean. When my room was a mess or my home or car was disorganized, I felt stress and chaos.

Fêng shui is an ancient Chinese system designed to improve our lives by orienting our physical spaces to take advantage of this positive energy. It is believed our home breathes as a living organism, similar to us. The thinking is that this life-force, or qi, enters our home through windows and doors and should be able to flow unobstructed around the spaces in the corridors and rooms. When this energy is blocked by clutter, our personal energy can become blocked, resulting in stress, anxiety, and even illness.

This belief is similar to the one I was exposed to as a child in the phrase, "cleanliness is next to godliness." Although I am not aware of a specific verse in religious text where this is stated, as a child and young adult being a clean person was emphasized. That included my body as well as my home and outdoor living space.

Today I realize that being clean pertains mostly to my behavior, thoughts, and language. But I have also learned that when my outer environment is neat and orderly, that organization spills over into my inner environment. Less clutter means less distraction, so my energy can be more focused and productive.

The positive benefits associated with maintaining a clutter-free and clean space are not something only I experience. People I am acquainted with who have a disorganized home, car, or work environment feel they have a disorganized life. Our surroundings reflect our mental state. When they worked to clean up and maintain uncluttered spaces, they began to feel less distracted, more organized, and more relaxed, and they experienced greater tranquillity.

Something I did to improve my mood and sense of well-being was to clean out my home and maintain clean spaces. This is especially important since I live in a world where collecting seems to be a widespread obsession. The chaos and stress of being surrounded by so much stuff can be distressing emotionally and physically.

At home I picked up every object and asked myself how I was impacted by it. Some of the items actually stored unpleasant memories, and keeping them around made me uncomfortable. If I did not love it or need it, or if it did not uplift my heart, I gave it away.

Taking an emotional inventory of my possessions also shifted something inside me. Releasing many of my things caused a beneficial change in some long-held patterns about what really mattered and made me content.

Another advantage of cleaning up our outer environment is greater inner awareness and respect for our shared outdoor space.

While we may have a home with a yard that we own or rent, the entire planet is our home and residence to billions of other people, animals, and plant life. It is a heart-responsibility to care about how our actions impact the planet and delicate balance within the natural world.

For example, in Los Angeles, owners must pick up after their pets—it's a law. I was out walking my dog when I overheard a woman comment that she did not need to pick up after her dog, because its droppings were good fertilizer. There was a time I thought my dog's poop was just fertilizer too; that is, until I took the time to learn and care about the environmental and public health safety reasons behind the law. Instead of assuming that pet waste is just good fertilizer it is responsible to keep ourselves informed about the laws and the possible reasoning behind them. Everything we do outside matters to the overall health of our Earth home.

I appreciate my little rescue dogs and have had nine so far. Each of them taught me to love unconditionally, to give without expectations, to bounce back from challenges, to not give up, and to be patient, purposeful, and present. Having pets in my life made me a better person than I would have been without their loving guidance. If you want a personal coach to help you learn to be your best, I highly recommend rescuing a live-in teacher.

Pets bring us joy and companionship, and having another form of life to share our home with is one of the best things we can do for our overall health and well-being. While our furry friends offer so many positives to make our lives fuller and more rewarding, we still have the duty to dispose of their waste properly.

The Environmental Protection Agency classifies pet waste as a pollutant, just as our own biowaste is considered an agent for both viral and bacterial diseases. So, pet droppings are not good fertilizer. Even if we do not live near a body of water, animal poop can get washed into storm drains and end up in faraway streams, rivers, and groundwater.

Part of loving ourselves is caring about how our environment feels and looks. There is a deep sense of balance derived from taking time to organize and clean out closets, drawers, bookshelves, tabletops, and cabinets. We determine whether the items in our home have a purpose and a place. We give away, donate, recycle, or sell any excess. Through the effort of cleaning up our home, office, and car, we can dramatically lessen distractions and improve our sense of well-being, balance, and inner peace.

This assessing and purging applies not only to our personal property but to the beautiful planet we call home. Take inventory of how you can properly dispose of paints, chemicals, printer cartridges, batteries, cell phones, computers, plastic bags, and other things in your everyday life that can negatively impact the natural world.

Leading with your heart is making thoughtful efforts to maintain clean spaces for everyone on the planet and all life that calls Earth home. The small actions we take do make a big difference. There is a healthy sense of pride and sense of accomplishment that comes from pitching in to be the change we want to see in the world.

MEDITATIONS AND EXERCISES

Sit down in a quiet place and write down your answers to these questions:

How do you dispose of everyday items such as paint, motor oil, antifreeze, or batteries that pose an environmental hazard?

Is there an area in your home, work, or car environment that needs to be cleared? If so, make a plan or ask for help to clean it up.

Try this exercise:

Take twenty minutes to organize your desk, clean out your car, weed your garden, or do some other straightforward, simple task. After you stop, ask yourself these questions: Did you find yourself going over the twenty minutes or quitting early? How did you feel before you started, during the process, and after you were done?

NOTES

Make Time to Play

"Regina, wake up! Pay attention."

Growing up I heard these words often. School was exceedingly boring in contrast to the world beyond the classroom. When the recess bell rang, I was the first one out the door. I raced into an environment where my attention was heightened and everything was vibrant and captivating.

It did not matter what activity was planned for the day. From kickball and baseball to board games, play released me from the captivity of the classroom routine. It gave me the delightful freedom to move and be amused.

On weekends I went wild for play. Piling into the car on Sunday afternoons, we took off with my best friend, his brother, my sister, and our moms. The winding road to the park reminded me of a snake weaving in and out of tall grass. Passing duck ponds, a golf course, and a rodeo arena, we arrived at a place without swings, slides, or merry-go-rounds, yet it was a playground full of adventure.

The unspoiled Rio Grande riverbank was teaming with opportunity. Thick vines cascaded from sturdy live oaks that lined the river's edge. Run-off channels rose from the river up to the street.

"I'm a pioneer!" my best friend exclaimed, scurrying up the gully on a mission to discover uncharted territory. Following quickly behind, I searched for wildlife.

It seemed only moments had passed when a car honk signaled the roundup to return home. Taking a final glance as our car reached the top of the hill, I realized it was going to be at least six days before we returned to the wonder of that playful place.

As a child, I was expected and encouraged to spend time entertaining myself in activities. Play remained a big part of my life as I grew into young adulthood, with softball, basketball, and other team sports. When I entered college, I continued recreational activities like tennis and volleyball.

As I moved into the world of work, home, and adult responsibilities, the activities of my youth were replaced with gardening and amateur landscape design. I enjoyed riding my mountain bike along wilderness trails, canoeing down the rivers of Alabama, and holding marathon card games with friends.

Then I got caught up in the race of life. Working too long and too hard to create what I thought was a successful life took its toll. Overworked, I was tired all the time, stressed, and consistently cranky. My relationships suffered because I was not budgeting any regular periods of recreational time.

One day I made myself take a break from the "all work and no play" routine. Taking my dogs on a long walk along the lake in a nearby national forest took me back to the days along the river with my friend. Memories of how it felt to be a child, regularly engrossed in playful activities, made me smile.

It was then I realized the time I took off from my busy life was not a waste at all. During the "down times" I get some of my most creative inspiration, renew my spirit, and feel relaxed and peaceful.

Today play is an important part of my life. I gather friends for cookouts and board games. I also enjoy gardening and birdwatching. Once a month I join friends for an outing to a museum or botanical garden. Three or four times a week I exercise at the gym. Each day around noon I take a walk through our neighborhood and spend time in the natural world.

Too often we get so caught up in the adult responsibilities of life that we dismiss the idea of recreational time with the belief that play is for children. Not true. Research suggests play is an important part of life, whether we are children or adults.

According to the National Institute for Play, "Play can dramatically transform our personal health and relationships, generate optimism, give our immune system a boost, relieve depression, foster empathy, and lessen stress."

Make time to play. Give yourself permission to be a child again. Permit yourself to return to a more innocent time in life, when doing something just for fun was encouraged and welcomed. No matter what activity you choose, do something on a regular basis to bring pleasure to your heart. Doing so is not a waste. It is a vital part of creating a joyful life.

MEDITATIONS AND EXERCISES

Sit down in a quiet place and write down your answers to these questions:

1. What do you do on a regular basis just for fun?
2. How can you incorporate more playtime into your busy life?
3. What are some ways you can involve family or friends in group play activities?

Tip: We are here to be joyful. If we are discontented, we must look to ourselves to find the reason(s) why, and then do something about it. Be your own Happiness Hero—no one else can do it for you.

NOTES

Spirit

I was standing at an intersection waiting to cross and noticed a young homeless man pushing a shopping basket filled with his belongings. He had a beautiful dog with him. Then I saw an older, well-dressed man approach the young man and kneel down to pet the dog. The young man was beaming. The dog's tail was wagging so fast I thought it would fly off, and the older gentleman was smiling from ear to ear. When he stood up I saw him hand the young man some money. They exchanged a handshake, and with one last pat on the dog's head the older man turned and walked away.

When I crossed the street I caught up to the older gentleman and said, "That was a very kind thing to witness. Thank you for what you did." He smiled. I smiled. For several days after I had a delightful feeling from witnessing such a loving act.

Each time you behave positively, regardless of how any other person chooses to act, you are aligned with the higher, wiser part of your being. When you behave in ways that align with your heart/soul/spirit, you create a life of joy and profound meaning.

The self-respect and control necessary to act from your heart come from loving yourself first. When you treat yourself with kindness, you have compassion for others. Giving and receiving with grace is necessary to exchange the intangible gifts of your spirit. Being grateful is fuel for your soul's satisfaction in life.

Love Yourself First to Love Others Well

Whom do you love? Whose face appears in answer to this question? Is it your husband or wife, a girlfriend, boyfriend, or partner? Is it your daughter, son, mother, father, a grandchild, best friend, or a beloved pet? Is it the Divine? Regardless of who causes your affection to swell, a truth to engrave on your heart about love is this: To love others well, you must love yourself first.

For many of my growing up years, I wanted to be a beautiful, popular person. Pretty girls and handsome boys got more attention, had more friends, were invited to more parties, and had more fun. It seemed those who were born good-looking were more important. That is what society, television, and movies led me to believe. But I was not pretty.

To make matters worse, it was tough growing up and not fitting into the mold of how I was supposed to dress as a girl. All my life I shied away from wearing dresses and skirts and girly shoes. Ribbons, bows, lace, and frill did not feel right on me. I did not want to be Miss America or have my hair curled.

Until graduate school, I was a below-average student in a world where getting As was valued so highly. Reading was not easy for me. Studying was not enjoyable. Mathematics beyond the basics was as confusing as a foreign language. I had no comprehension of chemistry or physics, and spelling, grammar, and writing were some of my worst subjects. The thought of taking an exam or having to dissect a poor little frog, much less a cat, made me cringe.

I was not attracted to boys, and I did not want a house with a white picket fence. I felt uncomfortable being programmed to value finding a husband, having kids, being a good wife, and doing what I was told. Who I was supposed to be, according to society, religion, and my peers, did not come close to who I really was. How was I going to survive in a world where I stuck out so much?

No, I was not beautiful. But I did take a dying chrysanthemum from my aunt's porch and replant it next to her driveway, where it thrived for many years. While on vacation with my family, rather than poke around a roadside trinket shop, I spent time giving water to a donkey tied up in the hot sun.

No, I was not a girly girl waiting to meet Prince Charming.

But as a little girl I asked my mom to buy shoes for a shoeless classmate, and I asked my dad for baseball equipment for the children at the orphanage.

No, I was not a superbrain. But I loved animals, flowers, the outdoors, and sports. Endless fantasies of being a superhero, defending the planet from evil villains bent on world domination, came more naturally to me. As a superhero, I would bring an extra sandwich to school for a friend who did not bring a lunch, rescue earthworms from the hot sun, take moths out of spider webs, and dry off little birds after they were caught in torrential thunderstorms.

Today I acknowledge that growing up I did not stick out at all. Born an average-looking, conventional, learning-challenged, jeans-wearing, gay tomboy, I was only uncomfortable being me, as billions of us are. I too was brainwashed into believing I was not good enough unless I lived up to other people's ideals and values.

Regardless of how hard I tried to fit the idea other people had for me, I failed—until one day I realized I am not meant to live another person's life. I am only meant to live mine. That is the day I became free to simply be me.

Taught to place the wants and needs of other people above my own, I learned the truth through resentment and disappointment. Loving ourselves first is not egotistical or selfish. It is responsible.

Love is more than a romance or devotion. Love is the state of aligning your behavior with the positive values of your heart. Loving yourself and others is expressing behaviors like sensitivity and forgiveness. To love is to be patient, honest, and enduring. But to show love's behaviors to others, you must first give love to yourself.

Have you ever told someone you love them in the morning, and then in the evening screamed at them? I have. It feels horrible.

I distinctly remember one occasion when after a long day of work I returned home to find the house in disarray. My partner decided to have friends over without giving me a heads-up. The kitchen was a complete mess. As soon as I walked in, I got hit with not only the surprising news but a request to help clean up and get ready for the guests that were to arrive within thirty minutes.

Without taking a deep breath, without slowing down to remember this is the person I love, I let her have it. This was not the first time I'd unleashed a barrage of negative comments, and sadly it would not be the last.

After that happened, I had a stern talk with myself. "Regina, how do you justify treating the people you 'love' badly? How can you tell your friends you love them and then treat them with disrespect or rudeness? How do you excuse telling family you love them, and then turning around and being dishonest or speaking to them harshly? How can you really show love to your pets if you are then impatient or rough, or you expect them to reason like a human being?"

An ego-illusion that causes us to suffer is the idea we are capable of suddenly becoming something we are not. If we are uncooperative and self-centered, it is not possible to instantaneously change into a cooperative and altruistic person when we meet Mr. or Ms. Right. If we do not value our body, our time, our individuality, being the best person possible, and being financially responsible, we are not emotionally equipped to support these values in those we care about.

Saying "I love you" is easy. "I love you" means someone is important to us. We would miss them if they were no longer in our life. We have affection for them. What is more challenging is to offer love's behaviors when times are hard. When people behave in ways that hurt or disappoint, or they continue to make bad choices and hurt themselves, our actions are put to the test.

To show love to both ourselves and others, we give the best of ourselves. This means remaining aligned with our heart by loving ourselves first.

Each of us is a one-of-a-kind miracle, distinctive among all other human beings on Earth. That means we were specifically designed to march through life following the cadence of our individual, internal drummer.

While the guidelines of our drummers are similar—be honest, stay positive, do no harm, be the best person possible, make the world a better place—the beats that compose our march vary widely. We may be gay, learning-challenged, or devoted to animals. We may be pushed by our parents to enter a certain profession. It may be one that does not make our heart sing. They may want us to be an accountant when we really want to be a health care worker.

We go against ourselves when we overrule what we discern is best for us in favor of satisfying others, fitting in, not making waves, or trying to be liked. Going against what we recognize is true for us results in regret, disappointment, and suffering.

One reason for our existence is to contribute something unique that only we can. Making our positive contribution becomes possible by loving ourselves first, through the action of remaining true to ourselves. Have you ever stopped to consider how special you are? Not from an egocentric perspective, but rather from the acceptance that you are truly one of a kind?

What an incredible gift it is to be an individual expression of life! What better way to recognize the value of the gift than by turning your focus from being the same as other people to passionately honoring your individuality?

There is no greater contentment than simply being you. Love yourself first by courageously placing greater value on the guidance of your heart than on what other people say is best or right for you. No matter how uncomfortable being true to yourself may be, there is nothing as satisfying as the self-love and self-respect you receive from steadily marching to your own rhythm.

No one, anywhere on Earth, is capable of being a better friend, confidant, and advisor to you than you. It is empowering to realize you can treat yourself as you want to be treated, support yourself as you want to be supported, and love yourself as you want to be loved.

Regard yourself with the utmost compassion, forgiveness, and respect. Look within to change feelings of helplessness and hopelessness into self-reliance and optimism. Focus on forgiving yourself and other people to repair the holes within your heart. Become familiar with what you value in life. Concentrate on being comfortable and content alone before seeking someone to share your life with. Stand up and cheer for yourself. Depend on yourself to create the life you want by being your own biggest fan.

When you make peace with yourself, you begin to live in peace with others. When you are your own best friend, you can be a good friend to others. When you have a kind and accepting internal dialogue, you can have a kind and accepting external dialogue.

Likewise, loving the Divine you believe in is truly possible when you love yourself. The Divine is the spark of holiness within your heart. The higher part of you is also the spark of life that connects all people, animals, and life in the natural world. Tenderly caring for, respecting, honoring, and nurturing yourself, other people, and the natural world is the way you express love for the Divine.

It's sad to think about, but people will come and go from your life. You are the only constant companion you will have from birth to death. You are and will always remain the most important person in your life.

The next time you are asked whom you love, see your own smiling face. When you love yourself first, you want to be your best, because the best of you is the only part worth sharing in your name as LOVE.

MEDITATIONS AND EXERCISES

Below are some behaviors of love. Place these actions within your heart to love yourself and others. These are the actions that give real meaning to the words "I love you."

Accepting: Amenable or open

Attentive: Mindful and observant

Committed: Carrying into action deliberately

Compassionate: Having genuine sympathy for others

Cooperative: Willing to work with others

Devoted: Characterized by loyalty

Empathetic: Understanding and being sensitive to the experiences and feelings of others

Encouraging: Inspiring with courage, spirit, or confidence

Enduring: Lasting

Faithful: Steadfast in affection or allegiance

Forgiving: Ceasing to feel resentment against an offender

Giving: Freely and without attachment putting something into the possession of another

Grateful: Appreciative of what one already has or has received

Honest: Free from fraud or deception

Kind: Of a sympathetic and helpful nature

Loyal: Characterized by unswerving allegiance

Nurturing: Helping grow or develop another person or animal

Patient: Steadfast despite opposition, difficulty, or adversity

Peaceful: Devoid of violence or force

Respectful: Characterized by or showing politeness or deference

Responsible: Marked by being accountable

Sensitive: Aware of and responsive to the feelings of others

Supportive: Upholding or defending, as in being an advocate

Tender: Marked by, responding to, or expressing soft emotions

Truthful: Sincere in action, character, and words

Understanding: Accepting tolerantly or sympathetically

Sit down in a quiet place and write down your answers to these questions:

1. What are some of the ways in which you are your own best friend? How can you be a better friend to yourself?

2. When have you gone against yourself to please other people? How did it feel?

3. What fears keep you from remaining true to yourself?

4. Aren't there things that you identify are right for you that make your heart sing? What are they?

5. Do you consistently give love's behaviors to yourself?

NOTES

Be Kind

Early spring in my neighborhood in Los Angeles is a heavenly time to lie in bed at night with the windows open. The orange trees in front of my apartment building are blooming. Orange blossoms, while fragrant during the day, become intoxicating at night. The sweet perfume wafts invisibly in on the light evening breeze and collects heavily within my room.

For such a powerful fragrance, orange blossoms are actually very small. One sunny day I spent thirty minutes picking up many of the tiny, paper-thin blooms that had fallen from the trees. Seeing them from below is deceiving. Only when I was squatted on the ground did I truly appreciate how little the flowers are. It takes quite a number of them to fill even the smallest package. But I carried on, determined. Squatting and kneeling under my orange trees, I picked up hundreds of blossoms, cramming them into a teeny ziplock baggie until it was bursting. I found a cheerful greeting card, put the sealed package of orange blossoms inside, and mailed it to my mother. With everything my mother has done in life, of all the places she's traveled throughout the world, she confessed that she had not once smelled orange blossoms.

As I sealed the envelope, I felt the excitement of her surprise at opening the card. Of her wondering for a moment what in the world I'd sent her. Of her opening the teeny ziplock bag, and for the first time breathing deeply, taking in the intoxicating fragrance, the smell of my love for her in the form of orange blossoms.

I've learned that acts of kindness provide me deep contentment. Knowing I helped brighten someone's day makes my heart feel full long after the event itself has passed. Thoughtfulness is the action that emotionally connects me to the people I know and also to people I may never meet.

Early on a summer evening I watched a car pull up and park

in front of my home. Without reading the posted parking signs, three young adults got out and walked up the street. Thinking they were possibly visiting a neighbor, I waited a few minutes to see if they returned with a parking pass. When they did not come back, I guessed they had gone to a local restaurant.

Although it was their responsibility to read the signs, I knew how I would feel if I returned from a fun evening to find a costly parking ticket. Instead of having them learn the hard way, I wanted to alert them to the parking restrictions through a positive experience.

As a resident, I am able to receive a special number from the police department that allows visitors to park. I called for the number and taped it to their car's windshield for the parking officer to see. I also left a note on the driver's side window that said, "I did not want you to receive a ticket, since there is no parking on this street after 6:00 p.m. without a pass." A few hours later, the car was gone. All that night and well into the next day, I had the amazing feeling that comes from performing an anonymous act of kindness.

Although we may never meet the people we help, being kind puts us in the position of understanding how others feel. Kindness is having empathy so we become enriched by another's happiness. And upset by another's anguish.

One day I found a dog wandering alone in my neighborhood. When I called the number on her tag, I got an answering machine. After I left a message with my contact information, I took the dog to my home.

Soon the phone rang, and an excited young man said he was on his way over. The dog and I went outside to wait. As the young man approached, the dog began to wiggle and bark. After clipping the leash to her collar, the young man turned to me with tears in his eyes.

"Thank you so much for finding Honey. I'm visiting my parents and the gardeners left the gate open. I didn't even realize she was gone," he said, as he reached out to hug me tight.

"You are welcome," I replied.

It was the best feeling, being in the right place at the right time to help reunite a pet with the person who loved her. Being kind sometimes results in creating a happy ending for someone else.

Each year my mom and dad's church holds an auction to raise funds for the community projects it supports. My father is an avid fly fisherman who enjoys tying his own flies. In preparation for the auction, my dad spent several weeks tying flies as his donation. Day after day, he carefully created the tiny lifelike insects, and when he finished, he gently placed each in its own section of a plastic box. In the end there were about forty of his handcrafted flies.

Before the auction, my mom told me about my dad's efforts. I secretly arranged with the auctioneer to be on the phone so I could bid. The big day arrived, and when it was time for my dad's item, I received a phone call. The bidding started at twenty-five dollars. Of course, I raised that to thirty dollars. It was countered at thirty-five dollars. I quickly bid forty. Apparently, someone in the audience wanted my dad's creations, too.

The bidding bounced back and forth between the two of us, until at sixty-five dollars I went for it and bid one hundred dollars.

"Going once . . . going twice . . . *sold* to the mystery caller on the phone," I heard the auctioneer say. He asked me to hold while he put my dad on the phone. No one in the audience, except Mom, knew who was on the other end of the line until I said, "Hello, Daddy. I'm so glad I got your beautiful flies." With that, my sweet father burst into tears of joy. He was so happy and surprised to hear it was me on the other end of the line. He turned to the crowd and said, "It's my daughter from California." The entire place erupted with applause.

It feels amazing to be in the position to surprise someone with a gift of kind-heartedness that touches both of you. Being kind creates lasting pleasant memories. Compassion and caring also create win-win relationships where both the giver and receiver benefit.

My sister and brother-in-law mentor inner city youth and provide a consistent motivational presence. After graduating high school, one of the young men they mentored decided he wanted a career in the military. They helped him enlist and were there to comfort him as he shared his reservations about being stationed abroad. They were the only people he knew to attend his graduation from boot camp.

Many times family is more a matter of heart than blood. Frequently the compassion and attention we share by being kind to those who enter our life turns out to be their single most important source of encouragement and influence. Someone who is treated with kindness becomes more likely to pass compassion and assistance on to others.

One day I took a walk along the Third Street Promenade in Santa Monica. Leaning against a stoplight was a young man of about twenty-five. He was holding a sign that read, "Help, please. Down on my luck."

He did not look up as I approached. I took five dollars out of my wallet, touched his arm, and said, "Here, take this."

When he did look up, he gently took the money and smiled. I noticed that his teeth were badly deteriorated—a sign of possible methamphetamine abuse. Yet within his pale blue eyes there was a familiar, alert presence.

I squeezed his arm and told him, "Respect yourself, you are worth it." He said, "Thank you. Your words mean a lot."

I kept my hand resting on his arm for a few seconds until the light changed, then I stepped off the curb and into the street. Halfway through the intersection, my tears began.

One significant heart-lesson I live by is that every soul is whole, no matter how wounded the human being. Lead with your heart and look beyond the outer human to clearly see and unconditionally love the soul within. Begin with yourself.

Each day you and I are given countless opportunities to express our good and charitable heart. Regardless of what form they take, the kindness and caring we give others not only help them, they also create positive energy that returns to us in so many different ways.

Kindness connects us to other people, reducing feelings of loneliness and emotional isolation. Caring and generous people attract giving people to them. By being considerate people, we will be liked by others.

Compassion decreases anger and depression and increases positive feelings and our general outlook on life. Being generous, affectionate, and nurturing promotes the release of endorphins that make us happy and calm and improve our sense of well-being.

Acts of generosity and empathy keep us connected to the emotional warmth of our heart. Not only does being kind keep us heart-centered, researchers have found that kindness makes our heart healthier, too, because emotional warmth produces hormones in the brain and throughout the body that help lower blood pressure.

Treating other people as you want to be treated is the foundation of all the world's religions and spiritual practices. There is a very good reason compassion is so revered. The energy we put out is returned to us.

Freely offer your shoulder for someone to cry on, your arms

to hold someone safe, and a friendly ear to listen. Each act of kindness you give will come back to you.

MEDITATIONS AND EXERCISES

Look for opportunities in your daily life to spread compassion, caring, and concern. It may be the hug you give someone needing a comforting touch. You may help a friend overcome a challenge, or encourage him or her to take advantage of an opportunity. Possibly you brighten someone's day with a phone call or greeting card. Maybe you offer encouragement by advocating for a cause close to someone's heart. You may be in the right place at the right time to come to the aid of someone in physical distress or to reunite a beloved pet with its human.

Sit down in a quiet place and write down your answers to these questions:

1. Remember a time when someone did something unexpectedly nice for you. How did it feel? (Be specific.)
2. Think about a time when you performed a random act of kindness that made someone else's day. How did caring for someone else make you feel?
3. In what ways do you show compassion to others? How do you treat yourself with compassion?
4. What are some ways that you can practice acts of kindness going forward?

NOTES

Freely Give and Receive

When I first encountered Ebenezer Scrooge in Charles Dickens' classic novel A Christmas Carol, I, like everyone, thought he was a despicable individual. He was rich and stingy, angry and miserable, seemingly without heart. He cared nothing for anyone except himself. Despising the poor and the hungry, he was a cruel boss who forced poor Bob Cratchit, his ever-loyal employee, to work long hours in horrible conditions, paying him almost nothing.

Scrooge was a dastardly man, but by the end of the tale he had become my hero. His complete transformation, from mean and miserly to kind and generous, left a deep and lasting impression on me.

The old Scrooge showed me that money, things, and power over others are not the source of joy and satisfaction. The enlightened Scrooge taught me that giving back creates joy and contentment in our lives.

While waiting to leave the Aerobus Central Norte bus terminal in Mexico City, I watched a man as he cleaned the food court. He alternated between sweeping, emptying the trash, and insisting patrons leave their trays on the table.

In the United States, customers of self-serve food stands are usually encouraged to return trays to a central location. Self clean-up is the primary method of keeping the tables tidy. After studying the man, I understood why he insisted people in this food court do the opposite.

When he found a drink cup with something left, he put it on a ledge, which was partially hidden from view. He carefully wrapped an uneaten part of a sandwich and a leftover package of french fries in a napkin and placed them inside a locked cabinet.

I was still watching him when I heard a commotion and shifted my attention to a young teenage boy. Dirty, barefoot, and in shabby clothing much too big for him, he asked people seated nearby for money. The food court man motioned for the boy to stop what he was doing and approach him instead. Taking the drink cup from its hiding place, he then reached into the cabinet for one of the napkin-wrapped bundles. Without a word, he smiled and handed both to the boy.

Over the next two hours, I witnessed several more disheveled and gaunt young people enter the crowded bus station. The man gave them whatever food and drink he had saved. The satisfaction he received from using the little resources he had to help hungry street children was evident with each smile and each pat he placed on their backs. The joy I got came from being in the right place at the right time to witness such a beautiful exchange of kindness and caring. I credit the generosity of the food court man for inspiring me to look for opportunities to give to others.

On another occasion, while taking out the recycling, I noticed a man digging cans out of the Dumpster. Internally, I heard a loving voice say, *Give him some money.* I went back upstairs and took the last nine dollars out of my wallet. I said, "Hello, my name is Regina. Please have this." He accepted the money and looked up to the sky with a big smile on his face with arms outstretched in a gesture of thanks.

"What is your name?" I asked, taking his hand in mine.

"I am John, but please, my hand is dirty."

"That is all right, John. I do not mind," I said as I shook his hand. "Have a wonderful day."

"Thank you," he said.

Not once did I think about what he might do with the money. Following a silent internal prompt, and without expectation, I gave what I had to help someone who did not ask, yet who gladly and graciously accepted. In return I received a deep sense of satisfaction and peace.

One day while eating at a sidewalk café in my neighborhood, I noticed a homeless man sitting nearby. I asked the waiter if he would take a menu to the man to find out if I could buy him something to eat, and he agreed. It made my heart sing to watch the man accept the food and water from the waiter.

Most often the occasions life presents for us to give are individual. We alone provide something to someone. And sometimes we have an opportunity to be part of a group that comes together in a common cause. Giving in numbers is a truly miraculous and mutually beneficial experience.

At Christmastime, my sister- and brother-in-law undertook a secret mission to raise funds to help save the home of a woman and her autistic son from foreclosure. They set a goal of $10,000 and spread the word by sending e-mails and personal letters to family and friends. They also made it clear all donations were to be from the heart and without the benefit of a tax deduction.

Each day I touched base with my sister to hear news of the progress. Day by day the excitement mounted. It was amazing to be part of the coming together of many hearts aligned to accomplish the goal.

Soon money from across the United States began to trickle in, becoming a steady stream. Small, medium, and large amounts began to add up. In the first week, the $10,000 goal was reached. In a week and a half, over $15,000 was received, and within two and a half weeks, over $22,000 had been donated.

Alone we may have the power to affect small financial changes in someone's life. When we become part of a joint effort for good, we can often just stand back in awe at the results. The power of several people joining forces for the power of good does indeed have the ability to change lives and the world for the better.

Giving of yourself and your resources to those whose need is greater than your own is emotionally and spiritually rewarding.

Lead with Your Heart

Regardless of if you act alone or as part of a group, the gift you receive for doing something nice for someone else is feeling nice about you. Helping others is one way you move past the "I" of ego and into the "We" of heart. Each time you help make someone's life better, you make your life better, too.

Your gift does not have to be money. Everyone has something to offer. You can volunteer time for a charitable cause, or read to the blind. You can give of your time to a homeless shelter, or mentor a child. You can also donate blood, deliver meals to the homebound, teach someone to read, provide transportation to a senior, or help a special needs citizen. Regardless of what form it takes, you experience deep satisfaction from giving back, and you leave yourself, other people, and the world better off.

And remember, not only did mean old Scrooge come to the realization of how good it felt to give, after many years of turning down his nephew's request to join him for dinner, Scrooge finally showed up and was received with a warm welcome. Scrooge not only learned the joy that comes from giving, but he also learned the benefit of receiving gifts from others, too.

To receive as readily as we give often means we must first address the notion, "It is better to give than to receive." I believed this for a long time. When someone wanted to do something for me or give me something, it was difficult for me to accept their kindness.

One day I realized that if it felt good to give to others, then when someone wanted to give to me, and I was reluctant to receive, I was in essence denying them the same good feeling. So, not being able to freely accept the generosity of others really told them, "I do not feel worthy." It was a wake-up call to realize that by not accepting freely I was actually insulting the person giving me the gift.

Because of that heart aha moment, I now receive as freely as I give. I appreciate the joy others get from what I give to them, and I welcome the joy others receive from my accepting what they give to me.

Leading with our heart is about living in healthy balance. One way we achieve positive balance is by accepting the joy that comes from giving and receiving.

MEDITATIONS AND EXERCISES

Sit down in a quiet place and write down your answers to these questions:

1. What are some ways in which you give back?
2. How would you describe the feelings you receive from giving back?
3. Do you receive as readily as you give? If not, why not? If you feel unworthy to receive, why do you think that is?

NOTES

Find a Reason for Gratitude

There was a time when my focus was on things I did not have. For many years, my glass seemed to be half empty, until I realized I was the one holding the pitcher. I changed my point of view from one of lack to one of gratitude. Through hardship and loss, I began to see life's glass was actually full to overflowing.

Dealing with physical pain over a long period of time wore me down. After a while, life was dull. I found less joy in daily activities, and the constant discomfort kept me on edge. Every day I woke up focused on the pain. Each evening I went to sleep wishing something would change.

When I received news that my twenty-nine-year-old cousin had been killed in an automobile accident, I experienced a dramatic shift in the way I viewed life. Physical pain turned into a positive sign that I was still alive. It was surprising to discover how much my pain decreased when my focus changed from living in pain to appreciating the life I had.

After being downsized from a job, I faced the daily temptation to just give up. Instead, I spent eighteen months getting up each morning with renewed determination. I became grateful for the opportunity to return to my parents' home, spend time with them, and help around the house. My father was dealing with bladder cancer. Being able to share these moments with him strengthened my resolve. My lengthy unemployment had a silver lining.

That lining turned gold when I found employment and drove through the gates of Berry College in Rome, Georgia, for the first time. The magnificent beauty of the campus was breathtaking. Its twenty-six thousand acres of trees, pastures, meadows, lakes, streams, cattle, sheep, and other wildlife were magical. I was instantly in love with the herds of small deer that wandered between the buildings as if they were a different kind of student. I was in heaven.

Although I have not worked for Berry College in many years, I am deeply grateful for that job. It was the opportunity that ended my unemployment. What a gift to have worked surrounded by such beauty in my last traditional job.

Gratitude for whatever happens in life—the positive and the seemingly negative—is my goal. For example, I appreciate the blind woman and her guide dog I met one day on the bus. She was smiling and contented as she softly stroked her handsome black Labrador. Thank you, gentle woman, for silently yet joyfully reminding me of my ability to see you, your dog, and our beautiful world.

Gratitude is feeling appreciative or thankful. The state of being grateful is the positive emotional acknowledgment of something you have already or are going to receive in the future.

Being grateful—for a sunny day, the food you have, a job, your partner, your pet, etc.—creates contentment, and appreciation for what you have gives you satisfaction. Being satisfied fills your heart with joy.

When you express gratitude, the act of being appreciative instantly connects you to your heart. Gratitude generates positive feelings: love, compassion, joy, and appreciation. When you focus on what you are thankful for, all stress, apprehension, and upset melt away.

Do you realize that the joy you receive from simply being alive is within your reach? It is true. All you need is an attitude of gratitude.

Slow down. Hug your loved ones. Take a moment to smell a rose. Feel the refreshing wind on your face. Enjoy the song of birds, the sound of water rippling in a creek, and the beautiful glow of dusk when the night creatures begin to stir. The more you find to be thankful for about life, the more life finds ways to appreciate you in return. It is the gratitude guarantee. Enjoy the little things, because the very best moments in life really are free.

MEDITATIONS AND EXERCISES

Here is an exercise that will help you connect with what you are grateful for in life:

Please get a pen and paper or your journal. Sit comfortably and take a few deep breaths. Draw air deep into your lungs. Take another deep breath, and feel your body relax. Continue breathing deeply.

A powerful action you can take is to make a gratitude list. Here are some simple questions to get you started. There is no hurry. Write as much as you want.

1. What are you most grateful for?
2. What are you grateful for now that you were not grateful for five years ago? Ten years ago?
3. What are you grateful for in regards to your physical body?
4. How have you turned a negative emotion into a positive, grateful one?
5. How has your heart led you to states of gratitude?
6. What lessons have you learned that you are genuinely grateful for?
7. Who has added value to your life?
8. How do you believe being grateful makes the world a better place?
9. What else can you think of to be grateful for?

Master the art of gratitude. Every day count your blessings. When you go to sleep at night, count your blessings. You are truly blessed.

──────────── **NOTES** ────────────

Lead with Your Heart

A Life Filled with Heart

When I was a little girl I loved superheroes. In comic books, movies, and flights of imagination, superheroes defended us mortals from villains bent on world domination. They fought for justice. No matter what personal adversities they faced, no matter how big the bribe, they remained committed to exposing the injustices of society. They did so while adhering to moral excellence. They lifted my spirits and sparked my imagination: What if I too had superhuman powers?

Superheroes are real. They are not only the superhuman subjects of fantastical stories, they are normal people. In fact, we are surrounded by them; they simply look different from how we imagine a superhero should look. They do not wear capes, or have X-ray vision or lightning bolts shooting out of their fingers. They do not stand out in a crowd, because they look like everyone else. They look like you and like me, and like our next-door neighbors.

Becoming a real-life superhero is much less dramatic than you may imagine. It does not require being bitten by a radioactive spider, or being caught in the blast of a gamma bomb, or being hurled to Earth seconds before your home planet explodes. You become a superhero by choosing to master yourself through developing a positive sense of purpose for each day, for life, and for how you personally make the world a better place.

You ask, If I take this action, what are the likely results? You care about the wake your behavior leaves. When you encounter the negative behavior of others, you refuse to ego-box or lower your standards by remaining steadfast in your commitment to stay fluffy (more on what I mean by "fluffy" in a minute). You defend the underdog by standing up for what is right. Time becomes a cherished companion and ally in creating your best life. And you heed the call to action by being the solution to help make your life and the lives of others the best they can be.

Care about the Wake You Leave

When I was young, I often went out on the boat with my dad. He liked to fish, and I enjoyed being with him. I adored the chill of the early morning air and the sunlight dancing on the water. I was in awe of my dad's skill as he took aim, casting the lure between the branches of a long-dead tree, now partly submerged in the water near shore.

To reach the magical spot I enjoyed, we first had to cross a big lake. My father made certain my life jacket was on tight. Then he pushed the boat away from the dock. Once we were safely clear, he put the motor in high gear and we were off, speeding toward our destination.

I did not enjoy facing into the strong wind created by the high speed. Holding on tight, I looked backward, observing the effect the boat had on the water as we raced over the calm surface. Spray shot up over the bow, wetting us. Buoys jerked up and down as we sped by. A flock of ducks quickly took flight, their tranquil morning disturbed by our waves. When we were closer to land, our boat's wake crashed hard against the shore.

After what seemed an eternity, we arrived. My dad slowed the boat down and turned the noisy, smelly, water-churning engine off. He moved up front to an electric trolling motor that silently propelled us the rest of the way, leaving only a small ripple as evidence of our passing.

As we moved slowly, without upsetting the wildlife, I delighted when dragonflies landed on the boat. Fish swam close by, undisturbed by our presence. Once, a bird came and sat for a brief moment on the steering wheel.

When it came time to head back, I became disappointed. Too soon we were off again, zooming across the lake, our wake disturbing the water and everything on it as we went by.

Many years later, during an especially hard period, it dawned on me: I am like a boat. I too leave a wake as I travel through life. Today, I choose to move at a slower, more purposeful pace, although I have not always selected the right speed and direction—in the form of responsible behavior—that represented me well to myself and the world.

There was a time when I behaved as a fast boat, churning up waves of drama and chaos that crashed hard over me and others. Many of the people I knew in that "former life" will confirm it. When I wrote a check that bounced, my embarrassment caused me to take out my frustration on the mean old bank. Running late, I aggressively honked at the cars in front of me or became impatient with pedestrians crossing the street. When I had loud parties, I ignored the impact on my neighbors. The plastic cup I carelessly threw in the gutter became part of a swirling mass of trash in the Pacific Ocean. Lying caused people to distrust me.

I now admit it because I was not genuinely proud, happier, or more peaceful for acting thoughtlessly. Life did not become easier or less stressful as a result of racing along without caring about the consequences of my actions. Life was most difficult when I behaved as if I were entitled to do as I pleased.

I was a junior in college when I overdosed on a combination of prescription drugs and alcohol. At twenty-one years old, I was sent to a psychiatrist. To deal with my "issues" he prescribed Stelazine, Thorazine, and Valium. Each of the bottles was clearly labeled with a warning about mixing the drugs with alcohol.

It was Valentine's Day, and a group of friends and I went to a popular nightclub. Before venturing out, I went to a friend of a friend's apartment. There I was offered a marijuana brownie, and I was so hungry I ate two.

We got to the club and I started drinking beer. It did not

take long before I was thrust into a waking nightmare. My body reacted violently to the dangerous mix of the prescription drugs, alcohol, and marijuana. I was sweating, having hallucinations, and my heart was beating so fast I was terrified it would burst.

I was rushed to the emergency room where I spent the night in the hospital. My parents were called, and the life I knew at that time as a college student was gone. I was forced to leave school and move back home. A year later I did return and completed my undergraduate degree.

Taking the drugs and choosing to drink was ridiculously stupid. But it was not the major mistake I made that night. Yes, I arrogantly dismissed any danger, thinking I was young and invincible. My egotism was also based on being completely inexperienced with drugs, alcohol, and marijuana. I now know marijuana was not the culprit. I have since smoked it without any of the side effects like the ones I experienced that night. But consuming it in such a large quantity is much different than smoking it.

Not thinking about how the drugs, alcohol, and marijuana could react together was completely irresponsible. But the worst lapse in my judgment was lying to my parents and countless other people after the event. I told everyone that someone had slipped something into my drink while I was at the club. The really stupid thing was that the doctors had already told my parents the entire story over the phone. It was a fantasy ego-illusion that I thought I could blame my irresponsible behavior on someone else and my parents would simply accept it with, "Okay, sweetheart." By not owning my behavior I had betrayed their trust. And I'd betrayed myself. In both cases once trust is broken, it is very hard to gain it again.

The sad truth is that I had told the lie of my Valentine's Day event so often I started to believe it. For years I was terrified of ordering a drink in a club or restaurant that I did not personally open, like a soda. Only when I accepted responsibility that it never happened in the first place was I able to earn self-trust again and to begin earning back the trust of others.

Ego rationalizes behavior after the fact. Heart seeks to determine the possible consequences before we act.

As a smoker I rarely considered the negative impact my cigarettes had on others. It was an ego-illusion to believe I was entitled to force my cigarette smoke on other people, children, or my pets. I also did not have the right to throw my cigarette butts and trash on a public street with the arrogant and immature expectation someone else is responsible for cleaning up after me.

The same was true about feeling I was at liberty to leave my shopping cart behind a car, or in the middle of the parking lot with the rationalization, "someone is paid to put it away," because I thought I was too busy to take a few extra seconds to store it myself. When I was financially irresponsible, I was not entitled to expect family, friends, the government, or strangers to bail me out.

Around age twenty I decided I wanted to buy a motorcycle. So I got a friend to cosign the loan. When I could not make the payments, the bank called my dad. He was furious over being asked to fix a problem I had created.

His upset was justified. I had not yet learned the value of a dollar, and that part of keeping my word is to be responsible for the financial commitments I make, namely to not purchase anything I cannot afford—even if that means saving the money to pay cash or at least provide enough of a down payment so that if times get hard I can still make scheduled payments.

In relationships, it was not responsible of me to project my fears and insecurities onto other people and expect them to remain a part of my life. Having a closed heart and being emotionally unavailable to someone and then becoming angry because I did not have a good relationship with that person was not fair.

It was inconsiderate of me to walk down the sidewalk texting or talking on the phone, oblivious of traffic and other people around me. When I was behind the wheel of a car, it was not okay for me to be aggressive with other drivers or pedestrians— even those who were slow. It was not my right to treat salespeople, restaurant wait staff, airline personnel, or anybody rudely.

Over the course of my life there have been many times I did not care about the wake my behavior created. The truth is that although I may live in a free country, I am not entitled to behave as I please! I am not free to do what I want without regard to the consequences of my actions. Action without accountability is not free. There are always consequences!

The more I allowed myself to push the boundaries of what is morally, ethically, and socially acceptable, the higher the level of negative payback I received. It was eventual and inevitable.

Extensive personal freedom requires me to operate at the highest levels of personal integrity. Doing so maintains my positive advantage within systems that often allow and encourage pushing acceptable boundaries to intolerable and ridiculous extremes. The notion it is suitable to act without caring about short- and long-term consequences is completely egotistical, motivated by the impatience, immaturity, and thoughtlessness of my self-centered ego.

Even though my name is Regina Victoria, I am not in line to any throne, or entitled to special privileges. What I receive in life—respect, good relationships, financial stability, academic success, and a good job—I am responsible for earning. A peaceful, joyful, and fulfilled life does not just magically appear. I must create it.

Then why had I felt entitled to behave in such irresponsible and self-centered ways?

Looking back, I realize my egocentric behavior was the result of some twisted idea that I was owed special treatment for being treated so badly growing up. I was angry at the world. I had been deeply hurt, and for many years I was self-centered, only concerned with my suffering.

Finally it dawned on me that I could not possibly be the only person who gets hurt, stressed, angry, abused, bullied, or ostracized. Other people also feel pain and deal with negative "life stuff." That open-hearted aha moment was what it took for me to stop seeing myself as separate and alone and to start seeing myself as one part of our Earth family.

I realized that each time I behaved without thought to the consequences of my actions I was leading with the selfishness of my wounded ego instead of the responsible values of my heart. Without holding myself accountable for my behavior, I did not pay attention to my feelings or actions. Instead, I operated on autopilot. I sped through life without thinking about the wake my behavior created.

At the time, I did not understand that it is impossible to have a contented life if I do not care how my carelessness impacts other people. A "me only" focus did not permit me to see I am not an island in the middle of the ocean. Selfishness does not allow for my being only one part of something far greater than I am alone. Leading with my heart, I realize that I am surrounded by countless other human beings and other forms of life. I am connected to them and need them to exist.

There was a time when we exchanged keys with a neighbor should we get locked out. We trusted each other.

There was a time when if someone needed help, neighbors rushed to be of assistance. We watched out for one another.

There was a time when if a child fell off her bicycle, a stranger walked her safely home. We cared for other people's children as if they were our own.

That time was recently, in my neighborhood, in the heart of the second largest city in the United States.

Good people are everywhere! You and I are part of a worldwide collection of human beings who are more similar than different. We are a human family, interconnected and dependent upon one another. So having an "us against them" attitude is not productive, peaceful, or loving. They are us and we are them.

Within my family are people who are African, Israeli, Palestinian, and Lakota Sioux, to name a few. When I include my friends, this adds people who are Egyptian, Iraqi, and Syrian, plus many more nationalities and cultures.

We practice many different faiths, including Buddhism, Christianity, Hinduism, Judaism, Muslim, Native American Church, shamanism, and spirituality. Some of us are atheist or agnostic.

A number of my family and friends experienced prejudice, internment at Auschwitz, persecution of ancestors, and other significant life challenges. Some are famous. The majority are not. Several are wealthy and highly educated. Some are not.

We are a group of individuals as unique as snowflakes and fingerprints. Yet, beyond skin color, personal history, and the outward societal measures of success, each of us is home to a heart filled with compassion, empathy, and wisdom that connects us. We are like M&M'S® candy. No matter the color of our outer shell, the sweetness of our heart within is the same.

It is our heart that allows us to feel the same mutual acceptance when we exchange a smile with a stranger, or to have the same sense of accomplishment when complimented on a job well done. Our heart allows us to feel the same emotions of joy, sadness, or exuberance for life, or to relate to one another's love for people, the natural world, and our pets. Our heart clearly comprehends that life on Earth is subtly connected and intricately dependent. One way to keep our heart open is to see ourselves in others.

True joy comes from creating and nurturing good relationships with everyone, not just our family and friends. Good relationships are not possible if we speed through life behaving as if we have a special pass to do whatever we want.

We are not superior to anybody else. Our time is not more valuable; we are not more valuable. A position of fame, power over others, or wealth makes us more accountable for leading with the responsible values of our heart.

Asking "How will it feel?" is the key which opens the door to our heart. Taking time to put ourselves in another person's shoes before we act allows us to be aware of how uncomfortable, frustrated, or lonely it feels to be on the receiving end of rude and thoughtless behavior. It does not feel good to be jerked up and down like a buoy. Being sprayed with or battered by the wake of another person's unconscious behavior is not enjoyable.

My actions create my life, and I want the best life. How I allow myself to behave is the true indicator of how much I care for and respect myself.

Yes, there was a time when I did not have the level of awareness necessary to recognize how my actions impacted other living beings. Today I realize caring about the wake I leave is what makes me feel fantastic about me. The gratification I receive from working hard to do the best thing for all concerned is more satisfying than another person's praise. Assuming accountability for my behavior results in my loving and respecting myself.

Doing the right thing is the right thing to do, because people of honorable character always finish first, even when we do not win the race.

When we have an argument with a friend, we apologize. Real friends care more for friendship than pride.

If we see someone struggling to open a door, we stop and offer to help. Helping others makes our life richer.

Smiling when we pass people on the street, at work, at the bus stop, or anywhere else makes our heart sing. When we send our heart out front to greet the world, it makes us content and others feel seen.

When we notice a car waiting to turn on to a crowded street, and we are in the position to let the person in, we do so. The time we spend allowing someone to go ahead of us is time well spent.

Experience life to your heart's content by letting your heart take the lead. Treat other people as you want to be treated. And remember, that does not mean waiting for them to do it first.

One day I was out walking with my dog, Madison, and I noticed a young man about sixteen coming toward us on a skateboard. Madison is scared of skateboards, so as he approached I bent down to pick her up. Just as I did, he hopped off the board and put it under his arm. I said, "Thank you." He said, "No problem. I realize some dogs are afraid of my skateboard." It sure felt good to be on the receiving end of his courteous behavior.

Our self-love and respect come from leading with our heart to care about our behavior. From being respectful of our neighbors, to being on time, to being a positive example of what to value and how to behave, we strive to be our best. We listen attentively and readily share our feelings. We speak to others with respect. We assume responsibility for healing our emotional baggage. We refuse to jump to conclusions about other people or speak of them unkindly. We do not accept hearsay as fact. We appreciate how good it feels to properly dispose of trash and lessen our impact on the environment.

At the end of each day, as the last thoughts filter through before sleep, we want to remember we did our best to be a representative of the finest humanity has to offer. Today we want to remember we made the world a better place for our being alive. Today we want to remember we were appreciative of the gift of life.

In gratitude for the gift of each day, we lead with our heart to create a living legacy of which we are proud. There is nothing naïve, submissive, or weak about supporting the ascendancy of our peaceful, courteous, patient, and responsible heart. True power is choosing to stop rushing through life without paying attention to our actions. Real courage is slowing down to keep our heart open to care about the wake we leave.

Enjoy life at a slower, more aware, and peaceful pace. Create a living legacy of which you are proud and for which you will be admirably remembered. You will positively impact other people and living things, which is a fine bonus, like getting toppings on the most delicious ice cream sundae of life for free.

MEDITATIONS AND EXERCISES

Sit down in a quiet place and write down your answers to these questions:

1. Reflect on how it feels to other people and other living things to be on the receiving end of your behavior. Does your behavior match your image of yourself? Explain how or why not.

2. How do you honestly feel about your own behavior?

3. What are some of the positive benefits you receive from caring about the impact of your actions?

4. Make a list of the people in your family, friends, and co-workers.

   a. What nationalities do they represent?

   b. What religious beliefs?

   c. What political beliefs?

   d. What are the things you have in common with these people?

--------------------- **NOTES** ---------------------

Stay Fluffy

As children, my sister and I had a pet rabbit named Honey Bunny, a tiny ball of soft, fluffy fur. She was cute, cuddly, and consistently calm. When I encounter a tense circumstance, or want to keep from being sucked into other people's negativity, I repeat "fluffy bunny, fluffy bunny, fluffy bunny" over and over in my head.

It really works. I let go of any frustration or resentment and cannot stay annoyed when I concentrate on a cute little bunny rabbit.

One day I was walking back from a neighborhood shop when I witnessed a driver stopped in the middle of the intersection, talking on her phone while presumably waiting to turn left. After the light turned red, she made a U-turn. Although there were signs indicating U-turns were illegal, she chose to do it anyway. Her SUV was too large to make it on the first attempt, so she had to back up and move forward repeatedly.

Drivers at the green light laid on their horns, while many of the pedestrians who were forced to wait on the sidewalk screamed at her. The woman gestured through her windshield with a rude hand signal, continued chatting on the phone, and maneuvered into the illegal turn to take a parking space in front of a certain store.

Throughout this incident I stood on the sidewalk, a silent witness to how the actions of one person inconvenienced and angered dozens of others. No matter how the woman behaved, or how those impacted by the woman reacted, I was determined not to allow the circumstance to ruin my good mood. I was focused on staying fluffy.

On another occasion, I was experiencing greater pain than usual from two previous back surgeries. I decided to consult an orthopedic specialist to see if anything could be done to alleviate the pain.

The specialist entered the room without introducing himself and quickly asked what was wrong. I began recounting the history of my back surgeries, as I had with other doctors. He interrupted me. "Do not talk to a physician that way," he said. "Wait until you are asked specific questions and then answer as quickly as possible. We are busy people."

I felt like I'd been hit in the chest. It was shocking to be treated with such blatant disregard—by anyone, but especially someone in a healing profession. So there was no way I was going to allow myself to remain open for further insult.

I took a deep breath and cut the examination short. Before leaving, I said, "Sir, I appreciate your time is valuable, but I am certain there are plenty of physicians who will be sympathetic to my needs as a patient."

I was shaking like a leaf the entire time. It is emotionally painful to be treated so rudely. Our fight-or-flight response kicks in. But no matter how shocking or arrogant the physician's behavior was, I was determined to stay fluffy. I've learned the hard way that if I had not, I would have felt much worse than I already did.

One day on the bus, a man verbally assaulted me after I answered his question of how many more stops until the one he wanted. I do not know why he began yelling at me about his being homeless. He was sure I didn't know "nothing about living on the street." Again the fight-or-flight instinct caused my palms to sweat and my pulse to race. I intentionally stayed quiet as the man stood up, took off his sunglasses, got a bit closer, and continued yelling. I concentrated on the cross around his neck, silently repeating *stay fluffy*, and thought to myself, *Do what Jesus would do*.

I smiled at the man who was yelling at me. He said, "What the hell are you smiling about." I calmly said, "I am looking at your beautiful cross." He barked, "Well I wouldn't know nothing about the Bible, or that kind of stuff." Then he left, moving loudly to the front of the bus and out the door, getting off at the wrong stop.

A young man seated next to me leaned over and asked if I was okay. "I'm fine," I assured him, finally able to breathe again. "He is not really angry with me. He just chose me to rage against because I am safe. Maybe it is my gray hair," I replied, smiling. Then I introduced myself.

Extending his hand, the young man said, "I'm Scott. It is nice to meet you, Regina. I don't know how you stayed calm and kind, but you did, and I'm impressed."

"Scott, there was a time when I would have taken the man's anger personally and verbally defended myself. But there was nothing wrong with how I behaved, so there was no reason for me to take his behavior personally. I just answered his question. How he chooses to behave is completely up to him. I learned the hard way when to keep my mouth shut, because there is no winner in an ego-boxing match."

It's hard being screamed at, but the angry, rude, and self-centered people we meet are a test. No matter how much we learn in life, the tests to see what we have absorbed do not end. I am so grateful to have learned that self-control adds much more to my self-worth and self-love than defending egocentric pride.

Occasionally you and I encounter people like the woman in the SUV, or the physician, or possibly a mentally unstable person, who are unconcerned with how their actions negatively impact other people. We can choose to take a deep breath, count to ten, and ask ourselves, "How does angrily ego-reacting to the rude, but not physically threatening, behavior of another person really benefit me?"

How other people choose to behave is their choice. You and I have the same choice.

Yes, we can be led by hurt feelings or wounded pride to impulsively fire something back, and there are many situations when it is appropriate and important to stand up for what is right. Yet, like in the case with the Dr. X college professor, when we egotistically call people on their own self-centered behavior, it is not likely they will say, "Wow! Thank you so much. You have allowed me to see how badly I acted."

Rarely, if ever, do situations with strangers like this turn out the way our ego wants. Few of us welcome being told when we have behaved badly. Many times we already realize our behavior is inappropriate. Even if we are embarrassed and ashamed, instead of stopping to question and assume responsibility for our behavior, we may instead allow our wounded pride to shoot the messenger.

Remaining positive and peaceful under stressful circumstances requires bringing a different level of awareness to the situation than that which creates it in the first place. I learned it is necessary to have a plan, something to focus on to keep ego from becoming caught up in nerve-racking situations or other people's self-absorbed behavior.

The next time you encounter someone who is rude, find yourself stuck in a traffic jam, or discover that someone has backed into your parked car, refuse to add any negative energy to an already uncomfortable occurrence. You cannot change an incident after it happens. You do not have the power to change other people or make them see things about their behavior they are not willing to accept for themselves. Instead, focus on behaving in a way you are proud to remember, by imagining something peaceful and calm that helps you stay fluffy!

MEDITATIONS AND EXERCISES

Write down your answers to the following questions and keep the answers handy for the next time you don't feel fluffy:

1. What were the feelings that arose when you chose to engage in an ego-boxing match with another person?
2. Describe a time when you refused to let someone's behavior bother you.
3. How would you describe the feelings that resulted from choosing not to ego-box?

Here is an exercise that will help you connect to your inner calm:

> Take a deep breath and relax. As you inhale, think about something that makes you peaceful. See yourself sitting next to a slow-moving stream in a forest thick with fragrant pine trees. Or envision the face of your child or loved one. Maybe the serene thought is seeing yourself curled up with a good book in front of the orange glow of a warm, crackling fire on a cold winter's night. Possibly having coffee with a friend in a little outdoor café brings you calm.
>
> Now, deep within your heart, feel the tranquillity that comes from being in your special place or with your loved one. Spend a few moments further decorating the scene to make your peaceful place come alive with vibrant colors, textures, and pleasant scents and sounds.

When life gets stressful or you encounter a situation or person that could ruffle your feathers, choose to come back to this memory.

Cherish Each Moment

The realization of how sacred a resource time is came to me on a rainy afternoon in a movie theater. The newly released film was horrible. The plot was thin, and the animated characters from a popular cartoon were now silly as "real" people.

Even so, I was torn about leaving. It was raining outside, and there was not much else to do on the gray Saturday afternoon. Plus I'd paid for the ticket and still had some popcorn.

After a few more minutes of wavering back and forth, I decided I'd had enough. Other people may have found it worthy of 114 minutes of their life, but I did not. I walked out less than fifteen minutes into it. Making the decision to do so was protecting the most important asset I have: my time.

Have you ever walked out on a mediocre concert or play? Passed up having dinner with someone who only talks about him- or herself? Declined an invitation to join friends for another day of sitting around doing nothing? Decided not to watch a repeat marathon of a favorite television series? Good for you. Time is the most cherished gift we receive and the most exquisite gift we can give.

Our time is our life. When we are born, we are given the gift of a certain number of minutes, hours, days, months, and years to live. Even though we do not know how much time there is to life, we do accept life has an endpoint.

The realization we will not live forever does not need to make us fearful of death. Nor does it make time an enemy. The idea we exist within an unknown, finite amount of time motivates us to treasure the gift of each moment. Leading with our heart, we choose to manage time with the same attention to detail as we do our finances.

You and I are the ones with power to determine how we spend

our time. If we feel rushed, and believe there are not enough hours each day to do all the things we think we must, then we must look carefully at what we really have to do. Maybe some of the items on our must-do list are not nearly as important to our overall joy and fulfillment as we assume. Consider the value of spending precious time in relationships, and in recreational activities to rejuvenate our body, mind, and heart.

Our career is an area to examine carefully. Maybe our current position takes too much time away from other, more emotionally rewarding areas of life, such as our children, our spouse, and our friends. We might even find our job objectionable, and therefore feel it is a waste of time.

One of the ways I established better time management skills was to make a list of the benefits of changing an overworked situation into one with a healthier balance between work and personal life. When I disliked my current position, I invested time wisely by taking the necessary action to make myself ready for a career in which I was motivated to spend time doing something worthwhile.

I also evaluated the time I invested in personal relationships. Our contentment is dependent on having positive and supportive relationships. If we are experiencing harm or abuse, or the relationship is just not going in the direction we desire, we must explore ways of improving it or preparing ourselves to move on. Cherishing each moment often requires having the courage to put an end to any relationship that does not consistently add value to our life. Time is life. Each moment is too precious to waste by arguing, holding grudges, being abused, or harboring disappointment.

We devote the precious moments of life to establishing and growing good relationships by being the best person we can possibly be. Then we seek out lasting relationships with others who are manifesting their best as well, so what we give and receive are in balance.

If our children run us ragged with activities, we figure out how to reduce their schedules to add more quality family time. A few outside activities could be exchanged for more time at home.

An important assignment we have as a parent, or person of influence, is providing positive examples. Look carefully at what our actions teach our children or employees about the importance of spending time wisely. Do we really want our actions to teach others to value anything over relationships?

There are 1,440 minutes in each day. Each minute is dear. Once it is spent, there is no way to receive a refund. We cannot purchase more. We cannot press pause on life to resume it at a more convenient time. Time is not a resource to be wasted, killed, or allowed to fly away from us without our being aware of where it went.

I realize what it is like to move through life so fast you lose sight of what is truly valuable. I also recognize this is not the way to create the happiest and most fulfilled life. Slow down. Spend the finite currency of your time wisely. Savor each moment, because it will not come again.

MEDITATIONS AND EXERCISES

Sit down in a quiet place and write down your answers to these questions:

1. If you feel overwhelmed, what activities can you let go of to create more balance and fulfillment in your life?

2. Does your job require too much of a time investment for you to have a healthy, balanced life? If it does, what are some ways you might improve that situation?

3. What are two ways you can create more time for recreational activities with family and friends?

4. If you find you are too busy, are there one or two group activities you would be willing to give up to create more time for yourself?

———————————————— **NOTES** ————————————————

Stand Up for What Is Right

Once, while walking my little dog, I had an encounter with a man who was out with his two large dogs, a Dalmatian and a Boxer. As they approached, I knew something was not right and picked up my dog, Madison. As we passed, the Boxer lunged at us. The man yanked its leash hard, then hit the dog.

While I do not engage in ego-boxing matches with rude drivers, unbalanced strangers on the bus, or arrogant physicians, there are times when it appropriate and necessary to stand up for what is right. Witnessing abuse in the form of bullying or violence is one of the times I do say something.

I took a deep breath and as calmly as possible said, "Please do not hit your dog, or anybody, for that matter. Unkindness does not accomplish what you want." He looked down and said, "You're right."

As I started to walk away, the Boxer got loose. I continued to hold Madison in one arm, and with the other I gently reached down and took the merely energetic and curious Boxer by the collar. Not once did I fear for our safety. I spoke softly to the dog, and when he was calm, I handed him over to the man.

On another occasion, I was waiting in the checkout line in a department store. The cashier was wearing a button that read, "Thanks for your patience. I am in training." She accidentally made an entry error on the cash register. She called the assistant manager, who quickly came to correct the problem.

While he was working to reverse the charge, he began sternly reprimanding her in front of waiting customers. We were somewhat surprised by the incongruence between her big red button and his impatience. Before I could speak up, another customer in line offered, "I believe each of us realizes what it is like to be new at a job. We do not mind patiently waiting. Do we?"

I joined the other customers in voicing our patient approval. The man turned to the cashier and publicly apologized. I will not forget the look on both their faces, and those of the other customers, at the exchange.

I remember watching a poignant television interview with two former high school bullies. The young man and woman cited the abuse they experienced at home and irresponsible, bullying behavior they viewed on television as the reasons they tormented others. What struck me was their revelation that not once in the entire time they were bullying did anyone reach out to help them. They both agreed that if someone were to have compassionately talked with them about their personal situations, it would have helped them gain some perspective about their behavior.

At the MacLaren Youth Correctional Facility in Woodburn, Oregon, young men are paired with homeless shelter dogs and supervised by professionals. Through Project POOCH, they learn the benefits of practicing patience and loving-kindness by taking care of, training, feeding, and bathing the dogs, as well as teaching them obedience. With this kindhearted approach, both the dogs and the youth offenders are successfully rehabilitated. The dogs leave the program ready for their permanent homes, and the youth reenter society with new job and personal skills, increased patience, compassion, and respect for other people, animals, and the natural world.

Kindness, patience, and compassion had the power to soften the heart of a man frustrated with his dog, an impatient store manager, bullies, and youth offenders. Using positive heart values to stand up for what is right also helped Mohandas Gandhi unite a nation.

Gandhi's peaceful revolution was actually inspired by Leo Tolstoy, widely regarded as one of the greatest novelists of all time. A nobleman of European aristocracy, Tolstoy was best known as the author of the realist fiction masterpieces *War and Peace* and *Anna Karenina*. He also was a moral philosopher whose ideas influenced Gandhi and Martin Luther King, Jr.

In "A Letter to a Hindu," written to the Indian newspaper *Free Hindustan*, Tolstoy argued that only through the principle of love could the Indian people free themselves from colonial British rule. Tolstoy identified acts of kindness, patience, and compassion as the right actions to counter violent revolution.

Inspired by the views of this world-famous writer, young Gandhi embraced Tolstoy's nonviolent standard as the appropriate model for him, regardless of what other people did. The resulting protests, strikes, and other forms of peaceful and passive resistance ultimately proved successful for Gandhi and India.

Remember Albert Einstein's wisdom, "Problems cannot be solved at the same level of awareness that created them." An important way we can positively facilitate change is to bring a higher level of peaceful awareness to our life situations.

Whether in personal relationships, dealing with criminal offenders, or seeking solutions to the global challenges we face, let us act based upon Einstein's wisdom. Let us use love to heal wounded hearts, faith to calm fear, peace to end conflict. Let us bravely stand up for what is right by spreading kindness, patience, and compassion whenever and wherever we can.

MEDITATIONS AND EXERCISES

Sit down in a quiet place and write down your answers to these questions:

1. How does it make you feel to witness other people being bullied or ridiculed?

2. When have you peacefully stood up for what is right in spite of resistance from others?

3. Can you remember a time when you brought a higher level of awareness to a situation? What were the circumstances? What were the results? To what other situations might you be able to bring that higher awareness? How might they change as a result?

NOTES

Be the Solution

This is an exciting time to be alive! So much is happening, and opportunities for positive change are everywhere. From the environment to how we treat each other and other forms of life, from rampant political corruption and global financial meltdowns to a seeming decline in social, decent, and honorable values, we are being forced to honestly examine issues that concern humanity's future and well-being.

You and I can see the seemingly unending stream of negativity and conclude that the world is going to hell in a handbasket. You and I can also expend our precious life-energy assigning blame, arguing the issues, shunning accountability, jockeying for power, maintaining the status quo, dreading the end of the world, or reaping profit from fear and misery.

Or, we can choose to be part of the ever-growing, worldwide collective of people who grasp this moment in time as their best chance to positively and peacefully address challenging issues that will result in the evolution of our individual and shared consciousness. We stop waiting, arguing, and pointing the finger of blame outward. We courageously and responsibly spend our energy by being an active part of the solution to clean up our messes and protect our Earth home and all who inhabit it. We openly and candidly challenge ourselves to change "business as usual" in all aspects of life. We assume personal liability for doing what we can each day to be a catalyst of change and raise positivism from what appears, on the surface, to be a sea of negativity.

You and I can begin to manifest the change we desire by finding an area of interest that makes our heart sing, where our skills are a good fit for making a constructive contribution. Join those expending energy by honestly evaluating the effectiveness and efficiency of our political and judicial systems. Become personally involved at the local level to ensure the best education for all children, to help reduce illiteracy, and equip them to deal with the issues we are leaving to their attention. Join a local environmental group and clean up our parks, cities, rivers, lakes, and streams. Assist in educating your community about recycling. Work with local animal shelters to bring the benefits of spaying, neutering, and adoption to our cities. Get involved to end hunger and homelessness. Serve as a mentor to an "at risk" child.

At home, remain aware of what you allow into your mind and heart as entertainment. Search out programming that inspires your intellect and supports the positive values you desire to see in yourself, your children, and our society. Send television and movie decision-makers incentives to develop positive, inspirational, and intelligent programming by turning off anything that insults your intellect or offends your values.

Seek impeccable reporting from news organizations you consult. Research the facts regarding current issues, rather than accepting editorial opinion and hearsay as truth. The time has come to use our brain.

Remember that beyond what advertisers want you to believe about what they think you want from life, the most valuable things are having family and friends, great relationships, enough to eat, a roof over your head, a healthy body, clean water, clean air, a healthy planet, healthy pets, and, foremost, living from the heart. These values are shared by countless people throughout the world. So, encourage others to live in alignment with what is truly important by no longer allowing media and advertisers to tell you what is valuable.

Scrutinize the organizations you entrust to foster your spirituality. Have the courage to question and move away from any organization or doctrine that perpetuates abuse, control, and fear or assigns responsibility for self-centered situations to something outside of you. Separate yourself from and stop supporting anybody whose personal agenda incites hate, negativity, blame, control, discrimination, ridicule, or rationalizations of those behaviors.

We are at a pivotal point in our development. The time has come to grow more connected to our wise, helpful, and intuitive heart. This is the part of us with the patience, discernment, and innovation necessary to help us have the best relationship with others, avoid problems, make life easier, and find the best solutions to what we face.

To motivate this part of us, we need to step away from the familiar and into the vast unknown of limitless positive possibility within our heart. We are not here to wonder what the future may hold. We are here to create the future we want, moment by moment, day by day. We have the ability to be the positive change agent we desire. We stop apathetically waiting for someone else to go first. There are no other people to go first. We are it. The time has come for us to become involved.

Our world is magnificently beautiful. Without a healthy Earth, we do not exist. It is not responsible to wait for some body of "knowledgeable people" to fix what is wrong with our planet. You and I must be the ones to take action.

There is no government, policy, or law that can effect greater change than you and I doing our part each day. Let's promise one another to care about the impact each of our personal actions has on Mother Earth. Let's join forces and clean up what we can of our planet. Together we will make a huge difference. You and I are the answer!

Let's begin by viewing challenges as opportunities to make positive changes. Let's agree there is nothing gained by continuing to view each other and what we individually and collectively face through a negative perspective. Let's accept there is no one responsible for coming to our rescue. Let's stop the self-deception that any group or governmental body operates on the enlightened level necessary to solve our problems for us.

We are capable of cleaning up our messes. We are best qualified to educate our children, stop overpopulating the planet, stop overfishing our oceans, end a dependency on environmentally destructive fuels, and accomplish any of the other items on our universal to-do list. Let us have faith that when the majority of us courageously lead the way in demanding a higher standard of responsibility from ourselves, the desire to rise to the higher standard will become prevalent.

You and I do have something vital to offer. We do have power to initiate positive change. The small actions we take daily do make a difference and will bring about the change we all desire. We are the solution.

Conclusion
Your Life, Your Legacy, Your Choice

The aroma of warm gingerbread cookies swirled deliciously around my granny. She was an excellent playmate, thrilling storyteller, and creative tailor of special items to outfit the fantasies of children.

When we skinned our knees, her gentle hugs were comforting. Spilled milk seemed to go unnoticed. There was never an angry, blaming word for a broken dish.

Granny was satisfied with life. Her glass overflowed. She accepted people as they were, laughed easily, and greeted each person with a smile. She did her best to enjoy every day to the fullest. Each of her children, grandchildren, and great grandchildren were convinced we were her favorite. She loved and was deeply loved. Yet her life was not easy.

She wanted to attend school but had to stop at the fifth grade because her family needed her to work. Granny was not wealthy, lost her teeth early, and lived with heart disease. She also faced the unimaginable grief of having to bury her five-year-old son.

Despite adversity, she did not dwell on or run from the disappointments of life; she courageously faced hardship by grieving, accepting, forgiving, and moving on. She made mistakes. But instead of living with regret, she made the effort to make a better choice the next time she faced a similar situation.

Granny was not afraid of death. She was focused on doing her best, each day, to live in ways she would honestly be pleased to remember. Eighty-five years of doing her finest added up. When she passed away, crowds of people came to pay their respects.

During her memorial service, her spirit was alive in the shared memories of family, friends, and acquaintances. She was praised for creating a life of joy and serenity. People were deeply moved by her humility, kindness, and friendship. Her compassion, trustworthiness, and faith were inspirational.

Each person with whom Granny spent time was touched by her open heart. Though decades have passed since her death, my memories of her have aged well.

When my other grandmother passed away, she did not leave the same memories. Her attitude was negative, her glass always half empty. Nothing was good enough. Life had been too hard.

She placed value on things. My memory of her surrounding herself with fine objects is especially vivid because I was not allowed to sit on the furniture in my grandmother's living room. I learned not to take it personally. Thinking back, I do not remember anybody ever sitting in her living room.

My grandmother also supported judgmental television evangelists. She sent them money and was especially generous with those who desired to change gay people into God-fearing heterosexuals. At the time, I took this personally. Later, I wondered if she may have felt differently had she known about me.

My grandmother's lifetime of self-centeredness caused her heart to close. Instead of facing life's hardships and challenges head on, she attempted to medicate them away. She was constantly ailing and focused on her suffering. As a result, her offputting demeanor kept other people at a distance. At her funeral, people struggled to find positive things to say. It was awkward and embarrassing.

Today, I realize how fortunate I was to know both of my grandmothers. While they were two different people, each taught me by her own example.

One grandmother modeled how to create a life filled with anger, resentment, and loneliness. She did not connect the dots between investing adversely in life and receiving the undesirable in return. She spent her life looking outward for accountability and change. When it did not come, she resorted to blame and increased efforts to control others.

The other grandmother was a positive role model who showed me how life works best. Granny understood she did get back what she put out in the world. She recognized part of loving herself was doing the work necessary to intentionally change any of her behavior that did not feel good to her or to others. She accepted that the greatest legacy we can ever leave is choosing how well we live.

How do you want to be remembered? I don't mean when you pass away and remain in the memories of those you leave behind. Nor am I talking about any intelligence, position, wealth, beauty, or power you may have over others. At the end of each day, how do you honestly, with your heart, want to remember about how you are choosing to live?

You and I were born in different places, raised by different people, with different experiences shaping our personalities, beliefs, likes, dislikes, and values. Beyond our diversity and the stories we can trade about less-than-perfect childhoods or traumatic life events, we are very much alike.

You want to love and be loved. You want to have deep relationships. You want to avoid problems and make life easier. You want to live a life of meaning. How can you live a life of meaning? By leading with your feeling and responsible heart, rather than being led by an unfeeling and egocentric mind.

You seek the most important part of something by getting to the heart of the matter. Putting your heart into something is doing your best, not from fear of punishment or expectation of reward, but rather for the personal satisfaction of a job well done.

Crossing your heart is promising to keep your word. When you are facing life's challenges, you have to have heart in order to remain aligned with the self-confidence and determination necessary to pick yourself up and carry on. As the home of awareness, heart provides you with perceptive wisdom.

From the bottom of my heart, I believe each of us is capable of regularly expressing from our attentive and kind side. For me, the journey began by confronting this limiting, egocentric thought: "I am only human."

There was a time when I believed ordinary people could not consistently behave extraordinarily, that reliably empathetic, honest, and conscientious conduct was only possible for famous, spiritually enlightened beings. Religious teachings, historical texts, and cultural stories elevate those who live as the greatest version of themselves to a place that seems incredible and often magical, making us feel less than worthy. Behaving as they do was desirable, but it was idealistic for someone ordinary like me. This is the real world, with real problems, real challenges, and real stress, after all. Then one day I challenged that thought with, *Who says this is the real world?*

By being in charge of my thoughts, I learned the greatest limitations I encounter in life are those I place on myself. I have said it is too hard, I just cannot do it, I do not have time, I am weak, I have tried and failed, it's easier said than done, I am poor, I am physically impaired, how I behave is part of my culture and beyond my control. Feeling unworthy, or thinking we are unable to align ourselves with the positive values of our heart, is an egotistical scoff at those who bring positive light and loving inspiration to the world.

Things seemed difficult until I made the decision to stop talking and start doing. Taking action despite the limiting thoughts allowed me to prove to myself that I was not weak at all, and that what I wanted to accomplish was not too hard, and persistence would lead to success.

The message shared by all who live honorably is this: We are no different than they are. We too can lead with our heart to live each day in ways we are proud to remember. Whatever we want to attain in life, our success depends on remaining optimistic and self-supportive. That means enthusiastically facing and overcoming the limitations we place on ourselves.

Today I am committed to living in a loving world, where kindness and patience rule my actions when dealing with problems, challenges, and stress. This is the real world I work to create for myself each day, moment by moment.

Accepting that the present moment is the only one in which I can take right action, I am confident that within my heart is the personal determination necessary to regularly behave positively. Purposefully setting my prideful ego aside, I can choose in each moment to avoid problems and build meaningful, loving relationships with my family, neighbors, co-workers, and the folks I meet each day.

The truth is, most people who value their greatest legacy— choosing, moment by moment, how well they live—do not achieve religious or historical acclaim. They are our grandparents, mothers and fathers, sisters and brothers, friends and acquaintances, bosses and co-workers. They are found in all occupations, in every age, in all races, in every country around the globe.

In response to the September 11th tragedy, a Maasai tribe of Africa donated not one or two, but fourteen cattle to the people of New York. To the Maasai, cattle are sacred, and their tribe's greatest worldly possession. To receive the gift of a cow from the Maasai is the highest expression of their regard.

Although this gift may be viewed as not especially useful to the people of New York immediately after the 9/11 crisis, the motivation behind the Maasai's selfless gift is impressive. Giving their prized possession to those whose need was perceived to be greater than their own comes from having hearts filled with enlightened empathy.

The Q'ero Indians of Peru, descendants of the Inca, live much as their ancestors have for centuries, on Ausangate Mountain east of Cusco, at an altitude of 14,000 feet. Q'ero elders preserve and share with their descendants a sacred prophecy of great change, or *pachacuti*. Similar to the Maasai, they believe moving the energy of loving acceptance across the planet unites people in the common purpose of caring for each other and for Pachamama (Mother Earth). Living a life of tender nurturing represents a heart-awareness of, and respect for, the connectedness of human beings and the natural world.

On HappyNews.com I read about a waitress who received a large check from a cantankerous patron who passed away. Regardless of how rudely the man treated her, she never took offense. Her enduring, committed, and giving attitude mellowed the old man. She became important to him. Addicted to her kindness, he visited the restaurant daily, always sitting in her section. In the end, he repaid her unwavering expression of having her heart in the right place in the only way he could.

Enlightened messengers teach that the reason for being is to make yourself and the world better off for your having lived. Accomplishing this goal means not only leaving an Earth-changing scientific, technological, financial, or cultural innovation as your legacy to humanity. While these may be invaluable contributions, the greatest achievement is controlling impulsive, self-centered, "I am only human" behavior to perform with positive, peaceful purposefulness in the countless actions that make up your day.

When you think about it, actions such as staying patient when caught in heavy traffic, remaining honest when given the opportunity to steal or cheat without being caught, or being kind to someone who is rude are how you live with love, compassion, and purpose. Each moment you set your heart on behaving with positive purpose, you align with the selfless, accountable, and caring side of your being. You rise above the limiting excuse that you are only human to lead with the best of your emotional, intellectual, physical, and spiritual self. You live as an ordinary person who creates an extraordinary life.

Those of us who choose to lead with our heart do so because we accept the truth that our behavior creates our life. We know conducting ourselves as sensible and kind people is where the potential for our greatest joy and fulfillment lies. Yet accepting the challenge to regularly act united with our heart requires overcoming a second limitation we place on ourselves: basing our conduct on how other people behave.

Many of us lose heart by believing if we do not aggressively protect ourselves, other people will take advantage of us, abuse us, or view us as weak. This may seem true to those who view power only as having control over people or things. But true power comes from within, and I believe deep down that most people are good. Good people derive their power from making the intentional choice to lead with the honorable values of their heart.

What you invest in life you get back. When you are accountable, kind, and calm, your life flows easily. Conversely, when you are irresponsible, cruel, and impatient, your life grinds to a halt. Self-centeredness separates you from other people. Egotistical actions take you out of the constructive flow in which relationships work best.

Meaningful lives come from establishing and nurturing good interactions with others. Remember, it is only possible for you to be one half of the association you have with another person. Your goal in any relationship is to be your best half—unless, that is, we're talking about the relationship you have with yourself. With that one, you are the entire union, and your goal is to be whole.

You become whole by choosing to create a life of positive meaning. Once that decision is made, you strive to live each day pursuing the goal. You own your behavior and care about the wake your actions leave. Each moment of life becomes a gift. You serve as gatekeeper to what you allow into your mind and heart. Communicating with care becomes a priority. You pay attention to what you are doing in the moment. Forgiveness releases you from anger and regret. You set healthy relationship boundaries. "No" becomes an okay word. Gratitude takes center stage over lack. You question what you believe, give as you want to receive, support others as you want support, and become the solution to leave our world better off for your having lived. The result of leading with your heart is the best possible personal relationship with you, and with other people who desire the same.

Upholding the standards you set for yourself will result in the worthiness, self-love, and acceptance you want. Leading with the unselfish, accountable, and sensitive part of you, there is no limit to what you will achieve. You will be joyful. You will have peace. You will live an ordinary life in the most extraordinarily memorable way.

You will live each day in ways you are genuinely proud to remember.

Namaste,

Regina

Acknowledgments

My heartfelt appreciation to: Leigh Davenport, Dorothy Randall Gray, Kara Knack, Kalpana Kulkarni Muzumdar, Cindy Nielson, Bill Simon, Nicole Stanton, and Chandra Sullivan for their time, loving support, and kindness in reviewing the manuscript in its entirety and providing input.

I am deeply grateful to Miguel Bravo for taking the images of love and strength I envisioned within my heart and making them come alive.

Words cannot express the depth of my appreciation to Eric Brandt and Tina Rubin for their editing expertise and the vital part each played in helping me transform my manuscript into this book.

I also want to thank Randy Davila and the publishing team at Hierophant Publishing for having the confidence in the manuscript to take up this project.

To each of the people named above, and to others not acknowledged here, thank you. This book was several years in the making and involved the support of countless numbers of friends, family, and members of the worldwide Romancing Your Soul community. The book would not have found form without the contributions each made to this process.

Bibliography

One of the most rewarding gifts we give ourselves is continuing to learn. Information is power. Knowledge pushes the boundaries of what we think we know and expands the understanding we have of ourselves, other people, and the world. It is by being informed that we are best equipped to make educated decisions.

I enjoy learning and continuously seek inspiration from many sources. Over my lifetime I have read hundreds of books and articles and listened to countless hours of lectures on a wide variety of topics. I am certain some of the knowledge I've gained from others has found its way onto the pages of this book, expressed in my unique voice. What follows highlights the specific books, articles, and websites I quoted from directly when writing *Lead with Your Heart.*

Question Your Beliefs

I'm not sure at what age children begin consistently saying no, but I am proud I did not grow out of that phase. As a result, I automatically question everything; not to make someone wrong and myself right, but to ensure that the highest, wisest, and most loving part of me approves of what I adopt as a belief.

Evaluation of my beliefs began in earnest when I was asked to blindly accept God as male. That just did not make sense to me, even as a little child. With the exception of seahorses, pipefish, and leafy sea dragons, for the majority of species on our planet it is the female of the species that births new life. So to my heart, it was not even common sense that God or a Supreme Being was male. If a divine being created the world, then it made sense that Creator is both female and male.

The belief that the Divine is both male and female is reflected in Judaism, which teaches that every person was created in the image of God (Ariela Pelaia, "What Do Jews Believe?" About. com, http://tinyurl.com/2dsupy4).

Hinduism, which originated several millennia before Christianity, also supports the view that God was intentionally placed into a certain form, including the male gender ("The Secret— Collection of Inspirational Quotes (Part 33)," PositiveArticles. com, http://tinyurl.com/q5krv38). So why did human attitudes and beliefs about the Divine change?

In Christianity, God became exclusively male when the ancient texts, originally written in Aramaic, were translated into Latin, German, and English (Michael Green, *Celtic Blessings: Illuminations*, Portland, OR: Amber Lotus Publishing, 2007). Although ancient religions originally favored the feminine, as human beings changed and evolved, so did their desires to dominate and control one another. When the males in power understood they could not bring new life into the world, they began controlling everything within their societies that was associated with women and the feminine (Leonard Shlain, *Sex, Time and Power: How Women's Sexuality Shaped Human Evolution*, New York: Penguin Books, 2003: 337–39).

The divine feminine was intentionally crushed, resulting in the misogynistic view that still remains prevalent among male-dominated societies. However, modern religious scholars and leaders are returning to the inclusive attitude that arises from not putting God into a certain form (Barbara Brown Taylor, *The Luminous Web: Essays on Science and Religion*, Cambridge, MA: Cowley Publications, 2000: 48).

The same evaluation necessary to adopt a loving, inclusive belief in a genderless Divine also allowed me to rise above a bigoted, racist upbringing. Growing up in the southern part of the United States in the volatile 1960s, I could have easily fallen in line with groupthink. But my heart would not allow me to automatically discriminate against another person because of the color of his or her skin.

I was born white because of my ancestry. My black and Hispanic friends were born with darker skin because of their ancestors. Like our hair and eyes, skin color is biological and not a choice. Archeological evidence points to the earliest known Homo sapiens' remains being found near the Ethiopian Kibish Mountains. That means modern human beings originated in the Horn of Africa around 195,000 years ago, so all of our ancestors were black (ScienceDaily, "The Oldest Homo Sapiens: Fossils Push Human Emergence Back to 195,000 Years Ago," www.sciencedaily.com/releases/2005/02/050223122209.htm, published February 28, 2005, last accessed January 30, 2011).

Like all other animals, human beings' physical features had to adapt and change for survival (Ashley H. Robins, *Biological Perspectives on Human Pigmentation*, Cambridge, UK: Cambridge University Press, 2001: xi.).

Human beings have a long and violent history of discrimination against difference. No matter who is singled out—the intellectually and physically challenged, those suffering from genetic abnormalities such as Down syndrome, or simply those with different cultures, foods, or religions—there is a prevalent egocentric tendency to place ourselves in a superior position.

This remains true for those whose sexual orientation is different from what is considered normal.

It is common for those of us who are gay to know the truth of our difference from an early age. I did, and while I was subjected to endless persecution, deep within my heart I just knew being gay was how I was made.

When my sexuality was discovered, my parents sent me to a psychiatrist to change me. For the first time in my life, I received the support I desperately wanted. The psychiatrist informed my parents that I did not need changing, because I was born gay. Modern scientific evidence confirms there is no single factor that determines sexual orientation (J. Satinover, MD, *Homosexuality and the Politics of Truth*, Grand Rapids, MI: Baker Books, 1996). Being gay is not a choice someone simply makes. The road is too hard, the hurt and rejection too painful. To survive in a world where everyone around me was convinced God hated me, I had to depend on the loving wisdom that resided in my heart.

Although ancient religious texts support the condemnation of many of our differences, modern religious scholars such as Dr. Mel White caution us against taking literally what was written many thousands of years ago. Science now offers evidence that was not available at the time those texts were written. As our understanding of the biology and genetics of human beings changes, we must responsibly refuse to blindly accept outdated and wrong beliefs.

Master a Mind That Has a Mind of Its Own

As I was growing up amidst the dysfunctional beliefs of society, family, and religion, my mind latched on to every judgment and condemnation. The preprogrammed tapes of shame, guilt, and unworthiness played continuously. To survive the external and internal attack, I had to learn how to stop the negative mind dialogue.

While taking control of my mind and its constant thoughts was essential, I can also appreciate that the process of becoming aware of thinking (and the motivations behind our thoughts) is a skill each person of positive purpose masters. The concept that our brain can be intentionally changed is now supported by research conducted by the scientific and medical communities. Our brain is not rigid, as we once thought. While our mind may have a mind of its own, the thoughts it creates and focuses on are within our control (Marie Pasinski, MD, "Nurture the Miracle of Neuroplasticity," The Huffington Post, http://tinyurl.com/lfz6jer, last updated March 7, 2013).

Pay Attention to What Is Most Important

The corporate world in which I worked for many years was focused on accomplishing huge numbers of tasks within any given day. It was an unspoken expectation that, as a worker and eventually a boss, I would wear many different hats. The same was true of family life, with cooking, cleaning, and attention to pets and other people's needs. Too often I felt overwhelmed from being pulled in an impossible number of directions at once. But no matter how daunting the task, I was expected to perform the impossible; that is, to efficiently multitask.

No one told me how to actually accomplish doing so many things at once, or why they should be done at once, or even if it is humanly possible to do so. After failing repeatedly at trying to wear so many hats simultaneously, I began to realize I cannot multitask like a machine. The truth is, human beings cannot think about or do more than one thing at a time, no matter how much we are told this is how we must lead our lives (Claudia Wallis, "GenM: The Multitasking Generation," *Time Magazine* online, http://tinyurl.com/mld642k, published March 27, 2006).

Research on brain function and multitasking, even among the younger generations with whom multitasking has become an accepted norm, continues to reveal that human beings cannot efficiently switch between tasks the way a computer does, by time sharing. Studies prove we actually slow down, have higher instances of error, and end up wasting more time than if we concentrated on one task until finished (D. E. Meyer and D. E. Kieras, "A Computational Theory of Executive Cognitive Processes and Multiple-Task Performance: Part 1. Basic Mechanisms," *Psychological Review 104*, 1997a: 3–65).

Simply buying into the belief that we can and should multitask is not responsible. If we do buy into it, then we are also accepting the fallacy that we can pay attention to each and every thing we are exposed to on a daily basis. But the truth is, our ability to pay attention has not increased in proportion to the increase in distractions (Herbert A. Simon, PhD, "Designing Organizations for an Information-Rich World," in *Computers, Communication, and the Public Interest*, edited by Martin Greenberger, Baltimore: Johns Hopkins Press, 1971 40–41).

Understanding that our attention is a finite resource is vital to moving ourselves into the position of responsible gatekeeper of what we allow into our mind and heart. We are indeed influenced by our thoughts and opinions of others. We are also impressionable to the messages we receive through advertisements, movies, the Internet, video games, and pornography, including watching violence and the denigration of one another as entertainment. It's not a simple matter of telling ourselves it's just a movie and not real. What we allow in does impact us, either positively or negatively, by actually changing our brain (Norman Doidge, MD, *The Brain That Changes Itself: Stories of Personal Triumph from the Frontiers of Brain Science*, New York: Penguin Books, 2007: xvii).

About the Author

Regina Cates has one mission in life: she helps people connect to and lead with their heart.

Through the sharing of her own personal experiences, Regina communicates universal truths in a down-to-earth manner that everyone can understand.

But Regina's life purpose wasn't always so clear. Alone and depressed on her forty-third birthday, she found herself wondering why life had treated her so unfairly. This emotional bottom resulted in a profound shift in her thinking, and from there her commitment to personal responsibility was born.

Regina has not been a victim of anyone or anything since that day. She now teaches others the importance of taking responsibility for one's own actions, thoughts, and words, and how doing so will transform a victimized state of mind into one of power, purpose, and peace.

Regina's story and teachings have led to a massive social media following, and her Facebook page has hundreds of thousands of highly engaged fans.

Join Regina on her website:

romancingyoursoul.com

Or on Facebook:

www.facebook.com/RomancingYourSoul

Hier**O**phant publishing
books that inspire your body, mind, and spirit

Hierophant Publishing
8301 Broadway, Suite 219
San Antonio, TX 78209
888-800-4240

www.hierophantpublishing.com